how2become

How to Become a Teacher

www.How2Become.com

As part of this product you have also received FREE access to online tests that will help you to pass the tests to become a teacher. To gain access, simply go to: www.PsychometricTestsOnline.co.uk

Get more products for passing any test at: www.How2Become.com

Orders: Please contact How2Become Ltd, Suite 14, 50 Churchill Square Business Centre, Kings Hill, Kent ME19 4YU.

You can order through Amazon.co.uk under ISBN: 9781910602942, via the website www.How2Become.com or through Gardners.com.

ISBN: 9781910602942

First published in 2016 by How2Become Ltd.

Typeset by How2Become Ltd.

Disclaimer

Every effort has been made to ensure that the information contained within this guide is accurate at the time of publication. How2Become Ltd is not responsible for anyone failing any part of any selection process as a result of the information contained within this guide. How2Become Ltd and their authors cannot accept any responsibility for any errors or omissions within this guide, however caused. No responsibility for loss or damage occasioned by any person acting, or refraining from action, as a result of the material in this publication can be accepted by How2Become Ltd.

The information within this guide does not represent the views of any third party service or organisation.

Contents

INTRODUCTION

The first day of school is often an emotional and trying experience for our children. We send them off, complete with badly fitting uniforms and branded lunchboxes, into an environment that is full of people they have never met, and subjects they have never heard of before. All of this be can be extremely disconcerting. When this occurs, children look for a source of comfort. Where can they find this, you might ask? Well, it all starts with their teacher.

The role of teachers has changed considerably in recent years, and has become much more varied and challenging. Far from the disciplinarian figures of the past, teachers are now an inspiration and role model to the younger generation. With more and more skill expectations being placed on teachers; the requirements to join the profession are harder than ever before. Knowing your subject alone doesn't make you a teacher. Teachers need to have a rare combination of attributes, which make them ideal for the role.

So, what qualifications do you need to become a teacher? And how do you actually become one? In this book, we will answer all of your questions. Using our step-by-step guide, you can begin your teaching career early, and progress up the teaching ladder. And that's not all! We won't just be helping you to become a teacher, but we'll also show you how to become a GREAT teacher. This book is packed full of insider tips on everything from lesson planning to keeping discipline in the classroom. You'll find these tips in highlighted boxes, making it easy for you to flick from page to page, and find all of the best advice to guide you through your teaching journey.

By the end of our guide, you will be in a perfect position to start leading your own classes, and secure a position in a school or college. You will have a fantastic understanding of what it takes to excel in the classroom environment, leadership qualities and more.

The truth is that while anyone can become a teacher, not everyone is willing to put in the hard work to do so. If you are willing to push yourself, then you have an extremely rewarding career ahead of you. Whether you are a trainee, experienced professional or completely new to the industry, we sincerely hope that the advice contained within this book will help you to get to where you want to be.

Top Teaching Tips!

Nobody likes to sit through slideshows or boring lectures. Your lessons need to be engaging, fun and interactive. You want your students to actively participate in the lesson, rather than learning passively.

Chapter 1
Teacher Core Competencies

Teaching is about more than just teaching!

In your career as a teacher, knowledge will be your greatest asset, however knowledge means very little without other tools to back it up. Qualities such as leadership, time management and discipline will all go hand-in-hand with your knowledge, to form the basis of your teaching fundamentals.

Before you decide to become a teacher, you need to assess yourself against these qualities. This will help you to decide whether you are prepared for the commitment that teaching involves. In this chapter, we'll look in great detail at these qualities.

Let's start by looking at the **"core competencies"** of teaching. Core competencies refer to a set of qualities, which will separate the very best teachers, from the very bad.

Listening

Listening is incredibly important for teachers. Unfortunately, when you are placed in charge of a class of 30 students, it can be extremely difficult. There are so many voices in the classroom that many new teachers become overwhelmed by the listening aspect of the role. This applies when you are one-to-one with a student too. In order to teach, you must be able to understand what knowledge needs to be imparted, and in order to do this you must be able to listen. Whether you are teaching children or adults, it's essential that your pupils are asking questions about the subject, and learning from your responses.

Have a go at the short exercise below, to test out your listening skills!

Listening Exercise:

You are teaching a class of Year 4 pupils. There are 30 pupils in the class. The subject being taught is French. In the middle of the lesson, one of the students puts their hand up.

Mary-Anne: *'Miss, my Daddy said that we don't need to learn the French language because French people are stupid. Even though I know that cheval means horse, and vache means cow, and mouton means sheep…I don't live on a farm.'*

How would you respond to this?

Answer:

Your answer should have been somewhere along the lines of:

I would praise Mary-Anne for her excellent vocabulary, but use this as an opportunity to explain how and why discrimination is wrong. French people are not stupid, and I would make sure this is clear to her and the rest of the class. We learn languages in order to remove stereotypes, not encourage them.

Remember that listening isn't just about listening to what has been said. Listening is about understanding beyond what has been said. Particularly when children are speaking, they often talk about things that they might not have a complete understanding of, and therefore it is important to respond to them in a way that is positive and allows the subject to be discussed professionally and sensitively.

Relationship Management

The second core quality on our list, is relationship management. Relationship management is all about resolving conflict and disagreement, and encouraging a good relationship between the teacher and pupil.

Remember that, particularly when dealing with adolescents or teenagers, conflict is an inevitable element of the classroom environment. Not everyone can get along all of the time. As a teacher, it is your job to prevent this from escalating. You must be able to provide a calm and reasonable support base, and must be someone who can look objectively at issues – in order to manage and resolve difficult peer-to-peer relationships.

Have a go at the short exercise below, to test out your relationship management skills!

Relationship Management Exercise:

You are a Maths teacher in a secondary school. You have just started a lesson with a Year 10 class, and you notice that there is a lot of tension in the classroom. The issue seems to be between two boys – named Joe and Liam.

The two boys are sniping back and forth throughout the lesson. Halfway through, as you turn your back to the class, a fight breaks out. Joe leaps across the room, with a compass in his hand, trying to get at Liam. Although the rest of the class intervene, it is clear that the lesson cannot continue with both boys in the same room.

<u>What do you do?</u>

A – Put both boys on opposite sides of the room, and make sure the lesson continues as planned. It's important not to disrupt everyone else's learning.

B – Send both boys to the headmaster's office.

C – Send Joe to the headmaster's office.

D – Ask to speak to both boys after the lesson. Carry on as normal.

Answer = C. Send Joe to the headmaster's office.

The correct answer is C, send Joe to the headmaster's office. The reason that you should select this, and not B, is that the two boys need to be separated immediately. Joe, as the aggressor, should be sent to the headmaster's office first – he is clearly not in the right frame of mind to continue the lesson and is acting aggressively. His behaviour is unacceptable and therefore he needs to be removed ASAP.

Remember that good relationship management is also about recognising that sometimes, other people are better equipped to deal with the problem than yourself. In this instance, keeping the two boys together in order to try and resolve the situation would be a big mistake, and could lead to even more trouble.

Instructing

It goes without saying that instructing is an essential element of teaching. In order to become a teacher, you must be able to teach! That means you must be able to give clear instructions, impart your wisdom in a way that your pupils understand, and lead by example. It is no good having knowledge or behavioural skills, if you have no idea of how to apply them in the teaching environment.

The quality of your lessons will depend on your ability to deliver knowledge and information in a clear and concise fashion. The way this knowledge is delivered also needs to be engaging. You can be as clear as possible, but if your students aren't interested in the subject or aren't engaged by the way you are teaching it, then they won't learn much.

Have a go at the short exercise below, to test out your instructional skills.

Instructional Skills Exercise:

You are a classroom learning assistant, preparing for a career as a teacher. You have been assigned to a Year 8 Maths class, helping students with the topic at hand. As you sit down to help two boys, you hear the following conversation:

Neil: You do the homework last night?

Alex: Nah, you?

Neil: Pfff, it was way too hard.

Alex: Yeh mate, didn't understand a word of it.

What do you do?

A – Immediately inform the teacher in charge that the two boys haven't completed their homework.

B – Sit down and continue talking about the subject at hand.

C – Ask the two boys to clarify what they didn't understand about the homework.

D – Ask the two boys to speak to their teacher about not understanding the homework.

Answer = C. Ask the two boys to clarify what they didn't understand about the homework.

The correct answer is C. Instructional ability does not just relate to your ability to give instructions, but to recognise when they need to be given. In this instance, there is a clear example of when instructions/help needs to be given to students. You need to take the initiative, and help the pupils yourself.

Organisation

One of the most fundamental skills for any teacher to have is good organisation. Organisation will separate the good teachers from the bad, and many people would argue that this is actually the most important competency. Without good organisation, you will really struggle to succeed as a teacher, and this extends to time management.

The most common complaint from teachers is that they just don't have enough time to complete all of the tasks that they need to. Teaching is the ultimate time consumer. The classroom environment is extremely difficult to manage, students don't always pay attention and it's easy to get side-tracked by a discussion/ overrunning subject, or misbehaviour in the classroom. Likewise, you'll have enormous amounts of marking to do, and lesson planning, too. The latter will severely eat into your free time, and ensure that you are maxed out by your career.

With all this, you should be able to see that organisation is absolutely essential. You need to take an organised approach to your work, be disciplined, and understand what needs to be done and in what timeframe. It is inevitable that at some point in your career, you are going to feel overworked. It's important that you can minimise this as much as possible, in order to get the best out of yourself and your pupils.

Have a go at the following short exercise to test out your organisation and time management skills!

Organisation Exercise:

You are a teacher with a huge list of things to do before the end of the school day. Take a look at the list below and prioritise the items in the order that you think they'll need to be completed.

Item 1. Someone has broken a vase on the first floor corridor and there is glass all over the ground. The caretaker needs to be called to clean this up.

Item 2. After checking through submitted work, you realise that one student has failed to give you their homework.

Item 3. You are required to submit a review of a term-time holiday request, for one of your students. This needs to be submitted before the end of the day, or the student cannot go.

Item 4. You need to photocopy some sample exam question sheets, for your Year 11 History group. They are taking their exam in two days' time.

Item 5. The Head of Year has asked you to organise a meeting between two boys, one of whom has been accused of bullying the other.

Item 6. You have a set of practice papers to mark, that are due in 3 days' time.

Item 7. A student has been sick outside of your classroom. The caretaker needs to be called to clean this up.

How would you prioritise these items? Why would you prioritise them in this way?

1 –

2 –

3 –

4 –

5 –

6 –

7 –

Answer = If you are a safe, smart and sensible person, then your list should look something like this:

1. Item 1. Someone has broken a vase on the first floor corridor and there is glass all over the ground. The caretaker needs to be called to clean this up.

Explanation = This should be your number 1 priority, as it is a health and safety issue. Broken glass is a great danger to students and faculty.

2. Item 7. A student has been sick outside of your classroom. The caretaker needs to be called to clean this up.

Explanation = This is another health and safety issue. Not only is this unhygienic, but the floor could be slippery and dangerous. Therefore, you should make this a top priority. If you've already called the caretaker to clean up the glass, you might as well ask him to clean up the sick as well.

3. Item 5. The Head of Year has asked you to organise a meeting between two boys, one of whom has been accused of bullying the other.

Explanation = Bullying is an extremely serious matter. This is something that needs to be sorted ASAP, and therefore you should make it a high priority.

4. Item 3. You are required to submit a review of a term-time holiday request, for one of your students. This needs to be submitted before the end of the day, or the student cannot go.

Explanation = Since this is something that needs to be done by the end of the day, and could have a serious impact on the student, you should give this high priority.

5. Item 6. You have a set of practice papers to mark, that are due in 3 days' time.

Explanation = Although item 4 is due in two days' time, this is also something that could be done very quickly and easily. Marking papers takes large amounts of time, and therefore it is good to get started on this early.

6. Item 4. You need to photocopy some sample exam question sheets, for your Year 11 History group. They are taking their exam in two days' time.

Explanation = You would need to spend some time

photocopying, and although this is not a high priority, you still need to factor in how many photocopies you will need.

7. Item 2. After checking through submitted work, you realise that one student has failed to give you their homework.

Explanation = This is not a high priority. It is not a safety issue, and does not need a large amount of time to handle the situation. Therefore, this would be your last priority.

Lesson Planning

You will become extremely familiar with lesson planning as you progress in your career as a teacher. Lesson planning is absolutely vital. It will help you to stay organised, keep your classes on track, stay up-to-date with which classes still need to learn which material, and plan out every single day that you are teaching. The problem with this, is that lessons don't always go to plan. In fact, it's extremely rare for a lesson to go in exactly the way that a teacher wants it to. Classroom disruptions, overrunning discussions and slow students are all issues that will take away from the chances of your lessons running smoothly.

One of the great things about being a teacher is that no two days are the same. You will face a variety of different challenges, demands and questions every single day. Once you start planning lessons, you'll really start to understand why teachers get so frustrated when their pupils are talking or messing around in class. Every minute that you have to waste asking the class to settle down, or behave, is a minute that could have been spent teaching.

The other reason that lesson planning is important, is that it prevents you from running out of activities halfway through the lesson. No teacher wants to be caught with no material, but if the class aren't engaging, or whizz through the material faster than expected; then sometimes this can happen. Games such as Hangman are a really useful way of filling the spaces left by this, and are a great method of imparting useful knowledge and interacting with students.

So, how do you actually go about planning a lesson? There are a number of ways to do this, many of which we will touch upon in this guide, but for now take a look at the brief exercise below and see how you get on.

Lesson Planning

Below we have listed a typical 5-point plan for a lesson. Your job is to read through the stages of the plan, and then write down examples for each exercise. Remember that this could be any lesson, so feel free to tailor this to your specific subject, or be as generic as you want! We've filled in the first one for you, to give you some idea of how to answer.

Step 1. Preview. The first thing you'll do in your lesson, is to actually introduce students to the plan itself. At the beginning of your lesson, you'll provide students with an overview of what will take place. The reason that this is so powerful is that it shows students that there is a plan. It lets them know that you are organised, in control and have a purpose for the lesson.

A good example of this could be putting a couple of words on the board, and asking the students to explain the relationship between these words, before explaining briefly what you will learn and practice during the lesson.

Step 2. Beginning Exercise. Next, it's time to start the exercises. The best way to start your class is with a lively and interactive exercise which, in effect, warms the students up. Not only will this create a positive atmosphere, but it will introduce the topics to the class in a fun and engaging manner, and encourages communication between different members of the class.

In the box below, list some examples of how you might go about doing this.

Step 3. Main Exercise. Now, you can move onto the most demanding tasks, and main activities of the lesson. There can be 2 or 3 of these, depending on how much time you have for the lesson. Don't forget that after each exercise, there needs to be some room for discussion so that you can ensure everyone is fully grasping the subject matter. You also need to allocate time for you to go around the room and discuss things with the class.

In the box below, list some examples of how you might go about doing this. You should list at least one individual exercise, and one group exercise.

Step 4. Bonus Exercise. You could finish the lesson by instigating a bonus/closing exercise. This is something that you would ideally like to use, but could also skip out if time doesn't allow for it. It's always good to have a bonus exercise readily available, along with step 5, in case the class finishes all of the set work you have provided.

In the box below, list some examples of how you might go about doing this.

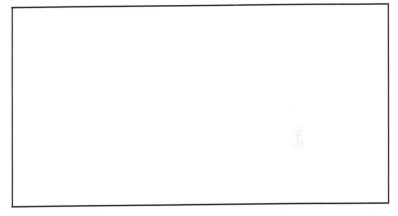

Step 5. Reserve Exercise. If even your bonus exercise is completed quicker than expected, you've always got your reserve exercise to fall back on. This should be an activity which isn't a fundamental part of the lesson, but could be used if everything else gets done.

In the box below, list some examples of how you might go about doing this.

Leadership

As the teacher, you are the leader of the class. You are someone whom students look up to, who they receive guidance from and will also act as an authority figure for the group. This means that you need to be able to live up to this role.

It's true that some teachers, when they start out, might struggle with this. Leadership isn't for everyone, and it's often difficult to deal with this at first. You might see yourself as a great teacher, but not necessarily a great leader, but the reality is that the two go hand-in-hand. Think about it like this. If you want your students to learn from you, and take on board the lessons you are teaching them, what is the best way to do that? The answer is with respect. If your students respect you, you'll have a far easier time teaching them. Leadership involves almost all of the competencies on this list, and is a fundamental quality for teachers to have!

Professionalism

When you are employed as a teacher, it is essential that you can act with professionalism at all times. Teachers are there to provide an example for their pupils, and therefore they must be able to look up to you. This means that your behaviour both inside and out of the classroom needs to be exemplary. You must be able to act with integrity, and show a good level of respect to everyone that you meet. As a teacher, an important part of your role is in practicing fairness and equality. Schools are extremely culturally diverse, and this means that everyone attending the school (staff or students) must be respectful of the differences between themselves and others, and treat every person that they meet in the same way. As a teacher, it's your job to enforce this, and show students the right way to behave.

So, why are these competencies important? Well, apart from showing you how you need to behave as a teacher, they will also be absolutely fundamental in the interview. As we've explained, the teaching interview is made up for 3 stages. The 2nd stage of the interview will not only test your knowledge of the competencies, but will require you to demonstrate occasions where you have used these competencies in the past. For example, you might be asked to talk about a time when you have demonstrated your organisational skills. In the interview section of this guide, we'll break down exactly how to do this.

Chapter 2
UCAS Teacher Training

The vast majority of postgrad teacher training applications in England are made through UCAS Teacher Training. This is a web based application portal, which allows you to connect with course and training providers. The application form that you submit will allow you to connect with:

- PGCE university or college course providers;

- SCITT training providers;

- School Direct, both salaried and unsalaried.

Application for training courses, which is known as 'Apply 1', opens on the 27th October, and allows candidates to apply for training programmes if and when they open. The majority of courses are done on a first come, first served basis. Therefore, you should apply as soon as possible in order to improve your chances of success. During Apply 1, you can apply for up to 3 different training providers.

The next stage is 'Apply 2'. This opens on the 9th November, and is for candidates who have not received any offers from the Apply 1 phase. Applications made during Apply 2 must be made one at a time, but candidates can keep applying until they are offered a place on a course.

Candidates who are applying will need to have 2 referees, and in the majority of cases will need to demonstrate that they have passed the Professional Skills Test. More on this later!

Now, let's look at the application form in more detail:

UCAS Teacher Training Application Form

The teacher training application form is split up into a number of different sections. Along with completing the standard questions regarding your name, address, personal background and ethnic origin, you will also need to complete sections on:

Your education

In this section, you will need to list your secondary and higher education achievements, and any qualifications that you have obtained so far. You should also list any qualifications that you expect to achieve before the training programme begins.

This section will include:

- Your GCSE results, A Levels and any equivalent qualifications. Your GCSEs in English and Maths are particularly important in this respect, and you'll need Science if you are applying to become a primary school teacher. Generally, you can use the UCAS search tool to find the requirements for each provider, which will help you to work out whether you have the qualifications that they are looking for.

- Your degree. It's important that training providers have as much information as possible about the subjects you have studied, and what type of degree you have (or expect to achieve).

- Whether you have passed the Professional Skills Test.

Your Highest Qualification

You will need to provide specific details about your highest qualification, or the highest qualification you expect to have.

For example, if giving details about your undergrad degree, then you will need to include each of the subjects that made up your degree, and then give each subject a percentage in terms of how important it was to the degree as a whole. This section is designed to help tutors assess whether your degree has covered enough of the subject to begin your training.

In most cases, the requirement is at the very least 50%. It's also extremely useful for primary course providers, where this section helps the assessors to identify whether you have any specialist teaching skills; which could be relevant to the subjects taught in their school. You should include courses and extras that you have attended in this section too. For example, modules which have enhanced your ability to take part in schemes being developed by primary schools, such as IT or environmental education.

Your Professional Skills Test

You will also need to provide details of the application process of your Professional Skills Test, with details such as:

- Your registration number;

- The date that you took the literary test;

• The date that you took the numeracy test.

Work Experience

In the next section, you'll need to give details about any experience that you picked up at school or in other jobs. You should do your best to demonstrate a wide range of experience, picked up across different jobs, schools and ages.

The application form will give you 500 characters to describe each section, and you'll also need to include the average time per week that you spent in each area/school/job.

This is a great opportunity for you to show that you have picked up and developed skills which could be useful in the classroom, such as organisation or leadership.

Personal Statement

The next section is possibly the most important part of the whole application. Your personal statement will have an enormous bearing on whether you are accepted or rejected by course providers.

The personal statement is your chance to show the providers exactly why it is that you want to teach, and why you would be suitable for their programme. In the latter, you need to show the skills you have and what you would bring to the course. This could be anything from practical experience to people management, leadership or communicational ability.

You can only create one personal statement, which stands for all of the choices made in Apply 1 and Apply 2, so make it count!

Let's look at a sample personal statement which exemplifies the above:

Dear Sir/Madam,

I am an enthusiastic, passionate individual who would love the opportunity to enrol on your course, as a trainee teacher. From a very early age, I have always wanted to teach. I have always been a leader, both inside and outside of the classroom, and this is just one of many reasons why I believe that I would be ideal for your course.

The foremost amongst these reasons is that I believe I have the skills required to make a success of myself as a teacher. Throughout my schooling and career, I have demonstrated my ability to lead different groups of people, on a number of occasions. I have worked as a project leader both at work and at university, and have always had enormous amounts of success with this. I am someone who is extremely good at managing people, maintaining a sense of calm and order when things take an unexpected turn, and have excellent communication skills.

The reason why I have applied for the PGCE is that I feel this is a programme which would be extremely suitable for my strengths. I am someone who greatly enjoys the challenge of the classroom environment, and would really embrace the theoretical side of teaching.

Furthermore, I know that the PGCE grants candidates with considerable opportunity to gain experience in a wide variety of placements, and this is something that really excites me. I can think of nothing better than jumping in feet first, and getting stuck into teaching.

In terms of work experience, I feel that the experience I've picked up over the last few years makes me an ideal candidate for this endeavour. I have spent time working as a volunteer in Ficshire Secondary School, where I assisted and observed members of the English department in their day-to-day working lives. This was a hugely beneficial experience. It was inspirational to realise that there is so much I have to learn about teaching than what I had already envisioned. The way that the teachers in the department went about dealing with their students taught me so much about how to behave in the classroom environment. I gained vital organisation tips, lesson planning ideas and people management techniques that I believe will help me to no end when teaching in a school. Above all else though, I gained the belief that I am someone who is truly capable of making a difference in students' lives. This is the main reason why I want to teach. The idea of educating and teaching, and turning young people into responsible adults; is extremely appealing to me. I want to make a genuine impact on the education of pupils, and this is the perfect way for me to do so.

I would be extremely grateful if you would consider my application for a place on your course.

Yours sincerely,

Now, use the space on the next page to plan/or write your personal statement!

Top Teaching Tips!

Set the tone. Discipline is fundamental in the classroom. Sometimes you need to lay out the consequences of bad behaviour early, to prevent misbehaviour from occurring. The more your students respect the rules, the better the learning environment will be.

Create your own personal statement

Referees

You will also need to provide two referees. Your application cannot be processed by UCAS until both references have been added, so it's important to ask these referees for their permission in advance. You'll need to explain your reasons for applying, so that if the course providers do decide to contact your references, the referees can provide good backing for your case.

Further tips for completing the application form

It's extremely important that you take your time when completing the application form. This is especially the case for the personal statement. If your personal statement is full of errors and grammatical mistakes, then it goes without saying that no school is going to take you seriously. You need to present the information in your form in as clear and concise a manner as possible, and check it several times for spelling errors. Our advice would be to lend it to a friend or family member to look over as well.

Make sure you keep on top of your contact details. If any of these change, then you need to update them on the page.

Many course providers will get in touch with you via the email address you have provided, so make sure this is an address that you always have access to and can check regularly.

It is possible to change your choices, but only within 7 days of submission.

Chapter 3
QTS And QTLS

In order to work as a teacher, you will need at least one of two fundamental qualifications. You can either qualify via the QTS qualification (Qualified Teacher Status) or the QTLS qualification (Qualified Teacher Learning and Skills). Once you have achieved one or both of these, you'll go on to complete an NQTS (Newly Qualified Teacher Status) induction year.

In this chapter, we will provide you with a full breakdown of each qualification, and the steps you will need to gain each qualification.

Qualified Teacher Status (QTS)

Qualified Teacher Status, or QTS, is the bread and butter qualification that every teacher in the UK will need in order to:

- Teach in a state primary school;

- Teach in a state secondary school;

- Teach in a state or non-state special school.

Teachers in independent schools are not legally required to have QTS or any other recognised teaching qualification, although most do. This means that if you want to teach at an independent school, you can assume that most of your competitors for the role will have qualifications to fall back on; meaning it's best to get some before applying.

QTS is awarded by the National College for Teaching and Leadership (NCTL), who act on behalf of the Secretary of State. The NCTL also awards QTS to other trained teachers, from the European Economic Area.

Once you have been awarded with QTS, you will be qualified to teach in any of the institutions listed above. After commencing employment, you will be subject to regular performance maintenance checks and paid under the school teacher pay scale. You can earn your QTS by completing a period of teacher training with an established provider/course. For example, by taking the PGCE. In this book we will cover a number of popular training routes for teachers.

Once you have completed your training period (detailed later in this guide), your training provider will send your results off to the NCTL, who will then award you with QTS. You'll be recorded on a database of qualified teachers, and will be able to access your QTS certificate via the college website.

Teacher Training Routes

There are a number of different ways that you can attain QTS. In this book, we will cover each of these sections in great detail. For now, take a look at the brief overview of each route, and think about which one might suit you best.

School Centred Initial Teacher Training (SCITT)

SCITT trainees spend the majority of their training period actually in schools. They work with pupils and experts in the field, to increase their knowledge and become better teachers. The advantage of this is that you can select from schools which are nearby. However, in order to complete the SCITT, you'll need to teach in different schools and take shorter placements in other settings/educational venues. You should apply for SCITT via UCAS Teacher Training.

School Direct (Salaried)

Trainees on the School Direct route will be actually employed by the school, and you will receive the salary of an unqualified teacher whilst you train.

In order to take the School Direct route, you must have been a graduate who has been working for around 3 years in any career. You'll be recruited by schools with a specific job in mind for them to do. The route takes around 1 year to complete.

Top Teaching Tips!

Part of being a teacher is about making connections with your pupils. Start talking about their interests, encourage them and take an interest in their lives. The better you can connect, the better they can relate to you.

School Direct (Tuition Fee)

On this route, you will train within a partnership of associated schools. In order to pay for this course, it will incur a significant cost, depending on the organisation that you are applying to. However, you may be eligible for a student loan in order to pay for this.

Assessment Only Route

The Assessment Only route is designed for candidates who already have a high level of experience working in schools or other educational settings, but don't yet have QTS.

Since candidates on this route already have a huge amount of experience, the Assessment Only route usually takes no longer than 1 school term to complete. You'll need to submit a portfolio of evidence, which will then be assessed against QTS standards, before being observed whilst teaching. In order to take the Assessment Only route, you will need to pay £2,675 plus VAT. You will also have to pay a further £200 upon attending the interview.

In order to apply for the Assessment Only route, you will need to apply direct to course providers. In doing so, you must have the full support of the school you are currently working at, as they will need to help provide evidence of your skills and supporting documentation. As you might have gathered, you'll need to have passed the Professional Skills Test before pursuing this route.

PGCE

The Postgraduate Certificate in Education (PGCE) is a full-time course, which normally lasts for 1 academic year. However, part-time options are available. The PGCE is an extremely popular option amongst graduates. During the course, you will attend theory-based classes at your university or college, and will also take part in at least 24 weeks of placement in schools.

Teach First

Teach First is a 2 year development programme, which is conducted in schools experiencing poverty or under-achievement. When taking part in this programme, you will be employed as an unqualified teacher, completing your PGCE in the first year and NQT (Newly Qualified Teacher) induction in the second year.

Furthermore, you'll be given the chance to gain a masters qualification. Applications to Teach First are made via their website. Recruitment is carried out on a rolling basis, with new places being made available in June. Teach First operates on a first come, first served basis, with spaces being filled once the right candidates are found. Later in this book, we'll provide you with all of the information that you need to know on filling in the Teach First application form.

Researchers in Schools (RIS)

The RIS programme is designed for researchers who are in the process of, or have already completed, their doctorates. As a trainee, you will be placed in a state school, where you will achieve QTS in the first year and NQT status in the second year. There's also an option to take a third year, which works towards the Research Leader in Education Award (RLE). In order to apply for RIS, you will need to complete the application form via their website. Later in this guide, we'll provide you with detailed advice on how to do this.

Professional Skills Test

In order to obtain QTS, you will also need to pass the Professional Skills Test. This is a test which requires teachers to demonstrate that they have the skills needed to fulfil their professional responsibilities within a school; rather than demonstrating their subject knowledge. The aim of the Professional Skills Test is to ensure that all teachers are competent in literacy and numeracy. Later in this guide, we will provide you with in-depth information on this assessment, including practice questions and answers.

> ### Top Teaching Tips!
>
> Teachers need to have thick skin. Children in particular can sometimes say things which they might not mean, so don't take it personally. Remember that they need a positive mentor!

Qualified Teacher Learning and Skills (QTLS)

QTLS stands for Qualified Teacher Learning and Skills. This is a professional status, which can be achieved by completing a professional formation. This is a process which allows you to put into practice the skills required for QTLS status. You can only attain QTLS via The Society of Education and Training. The benefits of QTLS include:

- When teaching in schools, QTLS is recognised as being equal to QTS;

- As a member of The Society of Education and Training,

you will have access to continuous developmental training, which will enhance your skills and further your knowledge;

• You will not need to serve an induction period in schools once you have attained QTLS.

Once you have attained QTLS status, it will be up to schools or local authorities to decide whether you are suitable for a post in their school. While QTLS does not guarantee a job opportunity, it does make you qualified to work as a teacher in schools across England.

The earliest that you can apply for QTLS is 6 months after you have received your ITE qualification. The professional formation initiative is designed to help current teachers show how they are developing, following their ITE programme. This means that evidence taken from initial teacher training programmes will not be accepted in applications.

QTLS Eligibility Criteria

In order to apply for QTLS, there are a number of criteria that you need to consider:

1. You must have a recognised qualification in teaching, at level 5 or higher

Applications for QTLS must have an initial teacher education qualification at Level 5 or higher. For example, a qualification that is equal/equivalent to a Diploma in Education and Training or similar. The Society of Education and Training aims its professional formations at teachers who already have a DET or PGCE certificate, however they also accept candidates who have equivalent qualifications.

-You can already be working in a school. If you are already in possession of a Further Education qualification, and are already working in a school, you will be eligible to apply for QTLS. Candidates must be able to show that they are in the continuous process of teaching students aged 14 or over.

-You can already have a PGCE and QTS. If you already have a PGCE with QTS, and are employed within the Further Education sector, you are eligible for QTLS. Similarly, if you are someone who has trained to work in a secondary school, and are currently in the process of teaching students aged 14 or older, then you are also eligible to apply for QTLS.

-Overseas qualifications. Candidates who have an overseas ITE qualification are also eligible. However, in order to apply, you will need to provide evidence from UK NARIC demonstrating that you have a teaching qualification of Level 5 or higher. You also need to provide a portfolio, which details your teaching experience.

2. You must have level 2 Maths and English qualifications

Applicants for QTLS must have both Maths and English qualifications, at Level 2 or higher. The list of qualifications which are currently deemed acceptable are shown below:

	ENGLAND, WALES AND NORTHERN IRELAND	
	ENGLISH QUALIFICATIONS ACCEPTED BY QTLS:	**MATHS** QUALIFICATIONS ACCEPTED BY QTLS:
L E V E L 2	• GCSE English A*-C (Language or Literature) • O Level English (Lang or Lit) – (1-6 or A-C) • CSE grade 1 English (Lang or Lit) • Functional Skills in English Level 2 and above • Key Skills Communication Level 2 and above • Level 2 Certificate in Adult Literacy • National Literary Test Level 2 • Literary Proficiency Skills Test • ESOL Skills for Life Examinations at Level 2 • Northern Ireland Level 2 Certificate in Essential Skills – Communication • Standalone English unit in a HNC or HND award • OCNW/OCN Level 2 GCSE equivalent in English • Certificates in Essential Skills (3800)	• GCSE Maths A*-C • O Level Maths – (1-6 or A-C) • CSE grade 1 Maths • Functional Skills in Maths Level 2 and above • Key Skills Application of Number Level 2 and above • Level 2 Certificate in Adult Numeracy • National Numeracy Test Level 2 • Numeracy Proficiency Skills Test • Associated Examining Board Proficiency Test in Arithmetic • City & Guilds Certificate in Maths Skills • City & Guilds Certificate in Maths Techniques • Essential Skills Wales in Application of Number Level 2 • NCFE Certificate in Basic Maths Level 2 • Northern Ireland Level 2 Certificate in Essential Skills – Application of Number • Standalone Maths unit in a HNC or HND award • Certificates in Essential Skills (3800)

	ENGLAND, WALES AND NORTHERN IRELAND	
	ENGLISH QUALIFICATIONS ACCEPTED BY QTLS:	**MATHS** QUALIFICATIONS ACCEPTED BY QTLS:
L E V E L 3	• A Level or AS in English Language • A Level or AS in English Language and Literature • A Level or AS in Communication Studies • IBSL Level 3 Certificate in British Sign Language Studies (QCF) • Signature Level 3 NVQ Certificate in British Sign Language Studies (QCF) • Welsh Baccalaureate Advanced Diploma Level 3 • Level 3 Certificate in Adult Literacy/ESOL subject support • Certificate in Delivering Basic Skills to Adults (City & Guilds Wales) • 14-19 Diplomas (Higher and Advanced) - England	• A Level or AS in Maths • Welsh Baccalaureate Advanced Diploma – Level 3 • Level 3 Certificate in Adult Numeracy subject support • Certificate in Delivering Basic Skills to Adults (City & Guilds Wales) • 14-19 Diplomas (Higher and Advanced) – must include Functional Skills Mathematics Level 2

ENGLAND, WALES AND NORTHERN IRELAND	
ENGLISH QUALIFICATIONS ACCEPTED BY QTLS:	**MATHS** QUALIFICATIONS ACCEPTED BY QTLS:
 L E V E L 4 • Degrees in English Language/Literature or Communication • Additional Diploma in Teaching English (Literacy) in the Lifelong Learning Sector • Additional Diploma in Teaching English (ESOL) in the Lifelong Learning Sector • Diploma in Teaching English (Literacy) in the Lifelong Learning Sector • Diploma in Teaching English (ESOL) in the Lifelong Learning Sector • Diploma in Teaching in the Lifelong Learning Sector (English ESOL) • Certificate for Adult Literacy subject specialists • Certificate for Adult ESOL subject specialists • Signature Level 4 NVQ Certificate in British Sign Language (QCF) • Certificate in English Language Teaching to Adults (CELTA) • Diploma in Teaching English to Adults (DELTA) • The Trinity Certificate in Teaching English to Speakers of Other Languages • Diploma in English Language Teaching to Adults (that are, or have been available from Cambridge (ESOL), Trinity College London and RSA	• BA or BSc or Bed or higher degree in Maths • Diploma in Teaching Maths (Numeracy) in the Lifelong Learning Sector • Diploma in Teaching n the Lifelong Learning Sector (Mathematics Numeracy) • Additional Diploma in Teaching Maths (Numeracy) in the Lifelong Learning Sector • Certificate for Adult Numeracy subject specialists

SCOTLAND			
	LEVEL 2	**LEVEL 3**	**LEVEL 4**
ENGLISH QUALIFICATIONS ACCEPTED BY QTLS:	• English Intermediate 2 • SVQ Level 2 • Core Skills Communication (Intermediate 2 and above) • ESOL National Qualification (Intermediate 2 and above)	• SVQ Level 3 (Highers)	• SVQ Level 3 (Advanced Highers)
MATHS QUALIFICATIONS ACCEPTED BY QTLS:	• Maths Intermediate 2 • SVQ Level 2 • Core Skills Numeracy (Intermediate 2 and above) • Scottish Certificate in Arithmetic (Ordinary Level)	• SVQ Level 3 (Highers)	• SVQ Level 3 (Advanced Highers)

How to Become a Teacher

IRELAND			
	LEVEL 2	**LEVEL 3**	**LEVEL 4**
ENGLISH QUALIFICATIONS ACCEPTED BY QTLS:	• Leaving Certificate (Level 4)	• Leaving Certificate (Level 5)	• Advanced Certificate • Higher Certificate
MATHS QUALIFICATIONS ACCEPTED BY QTLS:	• Leaving Certificate (Level 4)	• Leaving Certificate (Level 5)	• Advanced Certificate • Higher Certificate

EUPOPEAN AND INTERNATIONAL			
	LEVEL 2	**LEVEL 3**	**LEVEL 4**
ENGLISH QUALIFICATIONS ACCEPTED BY QTLS:	• European Baccalaureate • International Baccalaureate • University of Cambridge International GCSE English	• Trinity Integrated Skills – ISE 3 • Edexcel International Test of English (Pearson) – Level 3 • IELTS – 6.5 or above	• Trinity Integrated Skills – ISE 4 • Edexcel International Test of English (Pearson) – Level 4
MATHS QUALIFICATIONS ACCEPTED BY QTLS:	• European Baccalaureate • International Baccalaureate • University of Cambridge International GCSE Maths	N/A	N/A

If you obtained your Maths and English qualifications abroad, then you will need to supply evidence that confirms your qualifications are equal to or higher than a Level 2 or GCSE grades from A*-C. If you have not already obtained QTS prior to applying for QTLS, you will need to demonstrate that you have passed the Professional Skills Test.

3. Other teachers

If you are someone who already teaches English, Maths

or ESOL in the skills sector, then you will be required to hold a specialist subject qualification, which is equal to a Level 5 Specialist Diploma in Teaching, in Maths, English or ESOL.

4. Current practice

In your application form, you will be required to provide evidence of current practice, obtained 12-18 months prior to applying. Newly qualified candidates will need to show evidence of practice undertaken after becoming qualified. This will demonstrate to society that you are in the process of continuously developing your skills and knowledge.

5. A supporter/referee

You will also need a supporter, who will guide and support you through your professional formation. This person must be a qualified teacher, who has known you for 2 years prior to your application. Your supporter will provide comments on your practice and feedback throughout the QTLS process.

6. Society of Education and Training Membership

As QTLS is provided only by The Society of Education and Training, you will need to be a member in order to apply for professional formation. When applying, your membership must be up-to-date and sent along with a declaration of suitability form.

In the next section, we'll look at the UCAS Teacher Training Portal, and how you can maximise your chances of success.

Chapter 4
PGCE And SCITT

In this chapter, we will be looking at two of the most popular routes into teaching. These are the Postgraduate Certificate of Education (PGCE) and School Centred Initial Teacher Training (SCITT). Both routes are extremely accessible, and take only a short time to complete.

For this reason, more and more prospective teachers are turning to these programmes, which have enormous success rates.

In this chapter, we'll look in great detail at each programme and what they entail. Many of the tips contained in this chapter will also be relevant for School Direct (Fee Based) and School Direct (Salaried) so pay close attention!

What is the PGCE?

The PGCE is the best route available if you are someone who already has a degree in the subject that you want to teach. Possibly the strongest element of the PGCE is that it allows prospective teachers to conduct in-depth study of the theory behind learning and teaching, whilst still giving them a substantial amount of time actually teaching in schools, via placements. Once you've completed the PGCE, you will graduate with QTS, and will be qualified to teach in state schools within England and Wales.

The majority of PGCE courses start in early September, and take around 9 full-time months to complete (so about the standard length of 1 university year). In most cases, you'll be teaching a subject which links extremely closely with the subject that you did at degree level. However, it is possible to teach in a subject which doesn't link closely with this. If this is the case, you might be asked to take part in a subject knowledge enhancement course. This will be done before the PGCE actually starts, and therefore the route will take longer to complete. The courses generally run for between 2-36 weeks. You might also consider a subject knowledge enhancement course even if you don't feel it would be absolutely necessary. These act as a refresher, and will ultimately make your application much stronger.

The relationship between your degree and the PGCE will depend upon the type of PGCE that you are taking. If you are training to be a secondary school teacher, then you will need to demonstrate that at least 50% of your degree is relevant to the subject you want to teach (which has to be a part of the National Curriculum). On the other hand, primary school teachers will need to demonstrate a basic level/knowledge of all subjects; and your degree doesn't have to be a National Curriculum subject.

What is the SCITT?

School Centred Initial Teacher Training is a more direct route into teaching, which does not involve the same initial training/learning period as the PGCE. Instead, you'll go straight into a school, and learn on the job. You'll take your training within the school environment, and gain QTS at the end of it. The entry requirements for SCITT, and funding opportunities, are the same as those for PGCE courses. Likewise, applications for SCITT are made directly through UCAS Teacher Training. During your time on the SCITT, you'll be working in a range of different schools and will likely take a larger number of short placements than you would on the PGCE.

In a nutshell, the main difference between the SCITT and the PGCE is that when taking the PGCE, you will be given a period of initial learning and training at university. The SCITT is school-based and you will need to learn on the job. It's also harder to get places on the SCITT than the PGCE. Since the schools themselves will be delivering the training, there are limited places available. Despite the fact that the SCITT is more 'full-on' than the PGCE, you won't simply be thrown into the deep end and be expected to swim. You will be part of an established team, and just as on the PGCE, you'll receive extensive support from teachers and mentors. The school won't allow you to teach classes unsupported until they know that you are ready, so don't worry about jumping right in – you will have plenty of support and guidance along the way to ensure that you are more than capable of handling a class full of students.

In recent years, the above has all been included to incorporate School Direct, too. Many SCITTS offer School Direct courses. So, if you are an NQT (Newly Qualified Teacher), then this could be perfect for you.

School Direct

School Direct courses incorporate two different types of training route:

School Direct (Tuition Fee):

This is a hands-on programme which will provide you with access to high-quality training in top rated academies and schools around the country. The courses are designed by the academics within the institution, and are based around the skills that they are looking for in an NQT. You'll be recruited as a trainee onto the course, with the expectation of becoming employed by the school once a position becomes available.

This course incurs considerable costs on the part of the trainee. However, you will be eligible for a standard student support package, which includes bursaries and scholarships.

School Direct (Salaried):

This is a hands-on programme which normally takes around a year to complete. In order to qualify for School Direct (salaried) you must be a graduate who has spent 3 years in the world of work before application. It's not necessary to have spent 3 years working in a career related to education, but you must have some demonstrable educational experience or otherwise in the field to which you are applying. You should contact the schools that you are interested in working for, to ask about their recruitment arrangements. The quality of your grades could also impact on whether you need 3 years of work experience at all. Some institutions accept candidates who make up for their lack of experience with high quality results in other aspects.

Before Applying

Before you apply for PGCE or SCITT programmes, there are a number of things which you can do to make things easier:

Get some experience. While popular, you shouldn't really find it too hard to find relevant experience in a school-based environment. Most schools will be glad to have you assist or provide you with work experience, as long as you are enthusiastic and interested. The more experience you can get, the better. However, it's important that this has been in a mainstream state school and ideally you should have experience in more than one location.

Hone your organisation skills. This is not necessarily something which will lend to your application, but it's definitely something you'll need. It's common to find yourself overwhelmed with paperwork and lesson planning, and therefore you need to get organised early. Start buying folders and deciding how you are going to organise your work before you even apply. This will give you a great head start.

Research the course that you are applying to. For most people, the natural step will be to take the PGCE at the university where they have just completed their degree, or even attempt to do SCITT at their old school. However, this doesn't have to be the case. Regardless of where you are applying, you need to make sure that the learning style of the course is suitable for you, and it's also highly worthwhile checking out the local schools around the area. Although not always the case, the likelihood is that you'll be taking at least 1 placement in a school near you. If these are schools that you don't want to work in or don't like the sound of, then it might be worth applying elsewhere. Remember that teaching is a difficult and stressful commitment. It's important that you are taking the course/training in an environment where you feel comfortable.

Take the Professional Skills Test. While this won't apply to all courses, there are a number of course providers who will require you to have passed the Professional Skills Test before you can enrol onto the course. This is to ensure that they aren't wasting their time training candidates who don't have the mathematical and literary fundamentals needed to teach. If you are taking the test, then you'll need to revise thoroughly beforehand. Later in this guide, we'll give you a full breakdown of what the test involves.

The Benefits of the PGCE

In order to apply for a place on a PGCE, you will generally have to use UCAS Teacher Training. However, there are rare exceptions to this rule, where the universities and course providers will allow you to apply to them directly. In most cases, the course providers use UCAS Teacher Training as a simple way of processing the sheer volume of applications that they are receiving. Let's look at some reasons for why you should pick the PGCE over any other route:

Support Levels. While the PGCE (full-time) only

lasts for 1 year, one of the most popular elements of this programme is that it gives candidates a chance to prepare via classes and theory lessons; before being thrown into the terrifying classroom environment. Unlike programmes such as Teach First, where candidates are thrown straight into the deep end, the PGCE takes a slower and more patient approach to developing good teachers. Furthermore, you will be in the same boat as many people from your course; meaning that you'll have the opportunity to share ideas and support one another.

Freedom of choice. Another clear benefit to the PGCE compared to other options, is that you can (pretty much) choose the area/location in which you wish to teach. Although you might not necessarily gain a placement in the exact school that you want, and this will depend on vacancies/availability, you are extremely likely to gain a placement that is at the very least in your county. This in contrast to other programmes, where you can theoretically be sent to anywhere in the country.

Experience. The PGCE will provide you with plenty of experience in the classroom environment. As mentioned, you will take part in at least 24 weeks of placement in schools during the course. Combined with the theory side of the programme, this means that you are guaranteed time to get yourself familiar with the classroom environment.

Learning from experts. The theory-based element of the PGCE is one of the aspects that makes it so appealing to post-graduates. When learning on the PGCE, you'll be taught by professionals in the field, who have vast experience of teaching. The wisdom that these lecturers can impart will be extremely valuable. As a newcomer to the teaching profession, you'll learn to appreciate any tips or tricks that you can get your hands on, for dealing with your classes in the most efficient and professional way.

The Benefits of SCITT

As mentioned, just as you will with the PGCE, you'll need to apply for SCITT through UCAS Teacher Training. It is however advised that you contact the schools directly first, in order to gain as much information as you can about the programme itself. Unlike the PGCE, SCITT is a very full-on and immediate course, so it's best to learn as much as you can about whether this will suit you before applying.

Now, let's look at some reasons for why you should pick the SCITT over any other route:

Hands-on training. One of the most popular aspects of the SCITT is that it offers candidates a hands-on training experience. From day 1, you'll be working with experienced teachers at the schools themselves, learning straight from those who have seen and done it all. This is extremely valuable and a big part of the reason that SCITT has such high success rates. The SCITT is run by a professional consortium, who will be responsible for managing classroom assessments, observations and support.

Immediacy. For some people, the thought of sitting round in a classroom discussing how to teach; instead of actually teaching, is rather off-putting. If you are someone who prefers to jump straight into the deep end, and start teaching straight away, the SCITT route is perfect for you.

Variety. Unlike other programmes, the SCITT will require you to work in a number of different locations. While some people might prefer stability, there is a definite advantage to be had in teaching in different locations, to a higher number of different students. This will give you more experience than if you took the standard 3 placements offered by other training providers, and you'll be a stronger teacher for it.

Eligibility Criteria

In terms of qualifications, each course provider, university or school will differ on what they require from their candidates. You will be able to check the requirements for PGCE or SCITT applicants via the official university website, or via UCAS Teacher Training before you apply to them. When you are applying, you will generally need to meet two sets of criteria:

First, you'll need to meet the general course criteria. These are the fundamentals that the university or school requires from a candidate applying to train with them. These can be separated into primary and secondary. When applying, you might see something that looks like this:

Ficshire University General Requirements (Primary)

Applicants to this course must have an undergraduate

honours degree of 2:1 or above, from a UK-based university. We also accept a number of equivalent overseas qualifications. You will be required to attend an interview with a member of our faculty prior to acceptance on this course. You will need to have an extensive knowledge of the UK educational system, and must have demonstrable experience (3 days or more) of working in a UK-based school, before beginning your PGCE at Ficshire.

<u>Teacher Training is open for candidates who have:</u>

- A GCSE Grade C or higher in English Language, Maths or a Science-based subject. Ficshire does not accept English Language exams such as IELTS or Advanced Certificates as valid entry criteria.

- A degree that is related to a subject within primary education. This includes: English, Maths, Science, Art, Geography or History. You must have studied one of these subjects for your degree.

- You must also have an A-Level in one of these subjects, along with your degree.

Ficshire University General Requirements (Secondary)

Applicants to this course must have an undergraduate honours degree of 2:2 or higher, from a UK-based university. You will be required to attend an interview with a member of our faculty prior to acceptance on this course. You will need to have an extensive knowledge of the UK educational system, and must have demonstrable experience (5 days or more) of working in a UK-based school, before beginning your training at Ficshire.

Teacher training is open for candidates who have:

- A GCSE Grade C or higher in English Language, Maths or a Science-based subject. Ficshire does not accept English Language exams such as IELTS or Advanced Certificates as valid entry criteria.

- A degree that is related to the programme you are applying for. For example, if you are applying for the PGCE English, you'll need to have an English degree.

- GCSEs in English and Maths. If you are not in possession of this, you may be eligible to take internal tests. However, these can only be taken once.

- Secondly, you will need to meet the specific course criteria. This applies to primary school applicants too, especially if you are applying for a specialist position.

For example:

Ficshire University PGCE Primary Mathematics: Requirements

In order to take the PGCE Primary Mathematics, you must meet the general entry criteria, and the following:

- You must have a Mathematics qualification that is higher than GCSE level, for example AS or A-level.

- You must be able to show that you have used a

substantial amount of mathematics over the course of your degree.

Ficshire University PGCE Secondary Mathematics: Requirements

In order to take the PGCE Secondary Mathematics, you must meet the general entry criteria, and the following:

- You must have a degree in Mathematics, or a subject that is closely related to this. For example, engineering, physics, business or accounting. In order to take this course, you must be able to demonstrate that you have used a substantial amount of Mathematics in your degree.

- You must also be able to demonstrate that you have sufficient knowledge and experience of working in a UK secondary school. If not, you may be referred to take a Subject Knowledge Enhancement Course (SKE).

Subject Knowledge Enhancement Course (SKE)

As mentioned above, if your knowledge is not quite at the level that it needs to be to teach, you might be asked to take an SKE course with the aim of refreshing or enhancing your knowledge. This is generally a requirement for candidates who the course providers feel already have the right qualities for teaching, but need extra subject training before they do so.

Other reasons for taking the SKE include:

- If your degree wasn't in the subject that you are applying for, but in one that was closely related.

- You took the subject at A-level, but not at university.

- You have demonstrable professional experience, and the course providers feel that an SKE will help you to apply this to your teaching.

Unlike your tuition fees, SKE courses will be completely funded by the course provider, however you might be eligible to apply for a training bursary to support you whilst you take the course. Taking the SKE will slow down the progression of your course, as you'll generally need to complete this before the course starts, therefore delaying things. However, there are some providers who will allow the SKE to run in conjunction with your regular teacher training. The length of the SKE will depend largely on your personal learning needs. Some courses last only 8 weeks, but there are other more extensive courses which last for a full 36 weeks. Likewise, the style of learning in SKE courses can differ between providers. While most providers will offer the SKE as a full-time classroom-based course, others may require you to participate in the evenings or at weekends, or even take the course online.

Along with enhancing your knowledge, the SKE gives candidates a chance to really consider the subject they want to teach and how they can improve themselves as teachers.

On the next page, we'll look at some typical training modules. For the purposes of this, we'll be focusing largely on the PGCE.

> ### Top Teaching Tips!
>
> The end of the lesson is a crucial period. Take five minutes at the end of each class, to ask students to sum up what they have learned, solve a problem or practice what they've learned. Not only will this help them to remember, but it will show you whether your lesson has been effective!

PGCE Course Outline

In this section, we'll be looking at taking a PGCE course in much more detail. We'll run through an overview of the learning process, modules and what candidates will experience, before giving you a first-hand account of a full year-in-the-life of a PGCE candidate. The latter will be extremely useful if you are applying for the SCITT too, as this should give you a good indication of the type of things you'll experience while getting to grips with teaching.

Let's start by looking at a standard, 5 module course format:

The PGCE is generally designed to be extremely flexible, and will allow candidates a wide variety of choices in regards to the focus of their studies. Course providers recognise that trainee teachers have varying strengths, weaknesses and needs, and therefore the modules on the PGCE are designed to meet every candidate's developmental requirements.

When taking the PGCE full-time, each module will be worth a set number of credit points. Full-time trainees will complete 120 credits over the course of the year. In order to do this, your total hours of study will be longer than those of a standard university academic, taking a normal year of study.

The majority of the focus on the PGCE will be placement-based. This means that most of your learning will take place in the school environment. However, the course is organised in a manner which means that you'll gain vital experience and support via university-based sessions, before these placements start. This is known as professional study. You'll gain a clear understanding of academic expectations before being thrown into the classroom. You can expect to take around half of the modules during the year, rather than before the placements start. This is ensure that you have a manageable workload, and to allow for a progressive approach. In particular, the Professional Practice and Independent Study modules will run right up until the end of the PGCE.

Below we have broken down each stage of the course into phases, before breaking this down even further into 5 specific modules. Please note that this is a general overview of what you might expect to encounter. All courses are different in nature and format.

Stage 1: Induction

The induction stage of the PGCE is designed to help new pupils gain some perspective on the way in which professional teachers operate. You'll be provided with an introduction to pupils, schools and teaching theory; and will take part in lesson observation (via videos), essay-based analysis, discussion and subject specific research. Essentially, this phase will provide you with an insight into the way that children learn in schools, and how teachers help them to achieve this.

Stage 2: Teaching Beginnings

The next stage of the PGCE is where things start getting serious. In this phase, you'll be introduced to a wide variety of learning-based professional issues, and be given in-depth lessons on specialist subject development. The topics will focus on your ability to observe lessons, and react constructively to your own strengths and weaknesses. Throughout this stage, you will find yourself completing assignments to demonstrate what you have learned.

Along with this, you'll be given a brief introduction to placements in schools. You'll spend 2 days a week in schools, observing and helping with classes, before spending all 5 days in your final week within the school environment. You might be asked to teach on at least one occasion during these days, depending on the course itself. This is to give you thorough preparation for what is to come. The aim of this initial placement is to provide candidates with confidence in their ability as

a teacher, and to ensure that they are well on the way towards fulfilling the QTS expectations.

Stage 3: Improving Your Practice

The third stage involves equipping candidates with a more pronounced knowledge of their subject speciality, and the way they can incorporate their skills into teaching. This stage goes into more advanced detail about educational structures and how they benefit teachers and students. You'll be instructed on how to work within national qualifications, and will be given another placement in a different school.

As in the previous stage, you'll be spending 2 days a week within your placement; however on this occasion you'll be expected to take on more advanced tasks. At the end of stage 3, you will conduct a far longer placement in a school, consisting of 2-3 weeks at least. You will definitely have to teach/lead classes during this period, and this will be done under the supervision of a mentor/teachers already in the school. Along with this, during stage 3, you'll take part in more advanced professional studies. These will help you to develop new and extensive strategies for teaching your subject, and show you how to use vital resources in the most effective manner.

You'll need to complete an assignment which focuses on one particular aspect of your specialist subject, and teaching this subject. You'll also be given extensive lesson planning ideas, and gain an understanding of school-based assessment structures; such as GCSEs and A-levels.

Stage 4: Teaching Transition

Stage 4 is a crucial part in your PGCE course. At this stage, you will need to be able to demonstrate how your professional skills have developed over stages 1, 2 and 3 of the PGCE. You should be demonstrating skills and qualities which are in line with and will qualify you for Qualified Teacher Status (QTS).

At this stage of the programme you can expect to be spending large amounts of time in schools, and will be teaching and leading lessons by yourself. You will be expected to transition smoothly from trainee teacher to a teacher who is coming to grips with the learning environment. By the end of stage 4, the course providers will expect you to be teaching a wide variety of classes, and taking primary responsibility for the learning ethos of these groups.

Stage 5: Personal Reflection

The final stage of the PGCE is a period of personal reflection, with the view of enhancing your teaching abilities. You will spend less time teaching in schools during this period, and more time taking a final set of lessons/producing essays based on your personal development and skills.

You'll likely have to make presentations, discuss your strengths and weaknesses in great detail, and you may also be sent to teach in a third or fourth placement;

depending on the course provider.

Finally, once it's all over, you'll graduate with QTS.

Now, let's look in more detail at some of the modules that you'll take during the PGCE. You can expect these training modules to be highly similar in content to what you will be learning whilst preparing to teach in the School Direct or SCITT programmes. The difference is that you'll be taking them in a classroom or university-based setting, with fellow trainees.

<u>**Top Teaching Tips!**</u>

Keep a logbook of your classes. If you have time, write down the names of the students who participated the most during the lesson and those who participated the least. Use this information in your future lessons.

Module 1: Secondary Professional Practice

This is a module that you will take right at the start of your PGCE programme. It serves as an introduction to the role of a teacher, and aims to teach you core concepts such as taking responsibility. You'll learn how to teach responsibility to your pupils, and demonstrate integrity and professionalism both inside and outside of the school environment.

You'll learn different methods of working with your professional colleagues, with parents and carers, and external bodies.

The module aims to provide candidates with an understanding of theory, planning, and practical knowhow. You'll learn how to set expectations for students, how to monitor them in the classroom environment, how to assess students and you'll learn crucial behaviour management tips.

The overall aims of this module are as follows:

- To develop your personal skills as a teacher, and in the context of your subject.

- To provide you with the skills, qualities and attributes needed, to put your knowledge to use in a school.

- To learn personal evaluation skills, which will help you to improve your own teaching practice.

Module 2: Teaching and Learning

This is a subject-specific module, which will help you to develop your own knowledge and understanding of the key concepts of your subject. Candidates will look at how recent research and developments in the field could impact the material that they are teaching, essentially engaging in a subject-related study of pedagogy.

You'll explore different methods of communication, with the aim of ensuring that these methods are performed in a way that enhances the teaching of the subject. This module will teach you a wide variety of practical skills.

Essentially, you'll learn how to teach a lesson in your subject, how to control a class and deliver your subject related information in the best way possible. Upon completion of this module, you should find yourself in a position where you can lead classes in an exciting, engaging and vibrant manner.

The overall aims of this module are as follows:

- To develop your knowledge and understanding of the teaching specifications that are relevant to your subject.

- To develop your personal subject knowledge, and your ability to apply this when teaching.

- To develop your ability to reflect on your own practice, and make improvements.

- To develop your ability to critique and identify the strengths and weaknesses of resources related to your subject.

Module 3: Secondary Skills

This is a module which is based around personal development, critical evaluation, and theory. You will aim to fine-tune your approach to teaching and delivering crucial information to students, in order to increase the quality of your lessons.

The lessons delivered in this module will interweave with those in the previous 2 modules, and combine to form 3 essential modules for your future practice.

By using the lessons learned in all 3 modules, you will gain a solid platform upon which you can start delivering high quality lessons to students, and working in the school environment.

The overall aims of this module are as follows:

- To develop your ability to review and assess critically appropriate subject sources. To develop your ability to articulate and communicate when teaching.

- To develop your enquiry and questioning skills, helping you to better deliver information to students.

- To develop transferable skills, which can be used both inside and outside of the classroom.

Module 4: Teaching in the Wider Context

This is a module which aims to further the lessons taught in module 1. That is to say, you will be learning more advanced concepts about taking responsibility, interacting with colleagues in school and working with external people, such as parents/carers. All of this will go a long way to enhancing your professional development.

You'll focus particularly hard on lesson planning, teaching and managing the classroom. You'll learn key organisation techniques, advanced behavioural management concepts, disciplinary theory and how to form accurate assessments of situations and submissions. **The overall aims of this module are as follows:**

- To help candidates develop a deeper understanding of essential learning processes, which will help them to educate their pupils.

- To help candidates understand critical factors which could enhance and detract from their ability to teach.

- To help candidates develop their personal and professional classroom-based skills.

- To help candidates develop their ability to form positive working relationships and work as part of the wider school team.

Module 5: Independent Study

This is a module which encourages candidates to undertake their own critical reflection regarding their personal development. The module will require you to conduct a professional enquiry into your own progress and perform significant research into different teaching methods, theory and pedagogical techniques; all for the subject in which you have been trained.

You'll be required to use themes related to your subject, and to produce a research-based personal study of your approach to teaching. In this study, you'll evaluate your own practices, how they can be improved and what you have learned so far. All of this will provide the foundation for your journey into the world of teaching.

The overall aims of this module are as follows:

- To help candidates develop their own methods of enquiry and research.

- To help candidates reflect on their own teaching practice/methods, and implement changes based on what they find.

- To help candidates use academic sources, to improve their own methods of teaching.

PGCE Assessment

At this point, you are probably wondering how you are going to be assessed on the PGCE. You might be surprised to learn that there is no end of year examination. Instead, you'll be assessed throughout, on an ongoing basis, via observation of your teaching performance and via written coursework. In order to pass the overall assessment, you will need to demonstrate that you have the competencies required to be a teacher, and that you meet the Teacher Standard expectations.

Throughout the course, your university tutors and mentors will maintain a profile of your progress and achievements, and this will be used in a final report. Your final report will also be used as a reference for when you start applying for actual teaching posts. You'll have access to this progress report throughout the year, as a way of showing you what needs to be improved upon and what areas you are strongest in. The PGCE is all about helping candidates to become aware of what their next steps should be.

The coursework element of the PGCE is focused around submitting essays, based on what you have learned during the modules. You'll probably already have experience of this from your time at university. Below we've given two typical examples of essays that you might be set:

Coursework Assignment 1 = 2000 words

Produce an essay analysing the potential issues between a group of students/learners, and demonstrate how you would work to resolve and support those affected by these issues. In your essay, you should cover topics such as social and cultural difficulties. Your essay should demonstrate a clear understanding of the role of a teacher in the social spectrum of a school, and should make reference to key legislation and codes of conduct. Finally, you should ensure that your essay is adequately informed by research, reading and social theory.

Coursework Assignment 2 = 2000 words

Produce a critical examination and comparison between two key learning theories, and the implications that these have on classroom teachers. In your essay, you should cover topics such as behavioural assessment, classroom management and communicatory techniques. Your essay should demonstrate a clear understanding of both theories, and the way in which they can be applied within the classroom environment. You should ensure that your essay is adequately informed by research, reading and behavioural examples.

The coursework marks will go together with your observation results, to form an overall assessment. Once you've completed the PGCE, you will be able to use the points and status accredited by the programme, to take part in a master's course. The number of points needed for this, however, will vary depending on the university to which you apply.

Chapter 5
Teach First

In this chapter, we are going to explore the Teach First training route. We'll look in detail at how to apply, what the benefits of the programme are and what you should expect during the course.

What is Teach First?

Teach First is a charity-based training route that has really picked up in popularity over the last few years. Teach First select top graduate candidates and then train them in conjunction with a group of different universities. Candidates will then be placed in challenging schools around the UK, to work for a period of at least 2 years. To add to the challenge, you'll only be teaching in schools where more than half of the pupils come from the poorest 30% of families in the country.

The aim of Teach First is not just to train teachers to educate, but to train them to change lives. Since you will be working with low-income or struggling students, it will be your job to motivate them, help them believe in themselves and build a better future.

When working with Teach First, you will take 6 weeks of intensive training, before you begin teaching in one of the allocated partner schools. At the same time, you will be completing the Teach First Leadership Development Programme. We will cover this programme in extensive detail, in the next section.

Teach First has fantastic success results, with the large majority of candidates who complete the programme going on to teach. In some cases, Teach First doesn't just create teachers; it creates charity leaders, school governors and educational authorities. The aim of Teach First is to show candidates that education is a cause worth fighting for, and that your income should not prevent you from obtaining first rate teaching. It is this ethos which drives the course runners and applicants.

Teach First Leadership Development Programme

One of the most appealing aspects about Teach First is the Leadership Development Programme. This is a 2 year programme, which runs alongside your teacher training to help you learn business and personal skills, provide you with mentoring and gives you the chance to network and receive support from Teach First partners and members.

The aim of the programme is to teach you how to become an effective leader as well as a successful teacher. You will pick up skills which are extremely important in the classroom environment, such as adapting to difficult scenarios and learning what your biggest strengths and weaknesses are. You'll come to appreciate the value of caring about your students, and champion the Teach First cause, eliminating educational inequality.

You'll begin your Leadership Development Programme at the Teach First Summer Institute. This is a 6 week course which is designed to educate candidates on the challenges that disadvantaged pupils face, and prepare you for entering schools in September. The course takes place from June to August, and is a mandatory element of the programme. You won't be salaried during this time, but food and accommodation will be provided.

Before you attend the Summer Institute, you will be required to take part in Participant Preparation Work, known as PPW. You'll need to take an observation period in a school, read up on teaching theory and create a portfolio. This is not a piece of work that will be provided to you by Teach First, and you will need to do this independently.

Top Teaching Tips!

When testing students, prepare them first! Kids don't respond well to surprise tests. Show them how the test will be scored, give them the format and even try out sample questions first. The better prepared they are, the better they will do, and the more their confidence will grow.

The Benefits of Teach First

There are a huge range of benefits to Teach First. These include:

Unlimited options. As we've mentioned, Teach First doesn't just teach you how to teach; it teaches you to become a leader, and this is something that can be applied to a whole range of fields in the educational sphere. Teach First candidates go on to perform great things, that aren't just limited to the classroom. The values that Teach First instil on their candidates mean that the programme is creating a generation of teachers who want to go on and make an even bigger difference, through school governance and other important roles.

It's a fantastic cause. When you enrol in Teach First, you'll be working with students from some of the lowest income families in the country. This means that you'll be faced with a wide variety of issues, many of which are different to what you'll encounter in schools in other areas. You'll be a mentor to students who are in desperate need of it, and you'll have the chance to help them turn their lives around. What could be more noble?

You'll be salaried. Teach First candidates receive the basic salary for unqualified teachers in their first year, before this rises in the second year to the level of an NQT. Your wages will depend on where you are teaching.

You'll learn responsibility. Teach First is hard. You won't just be thrown straight into the deep end but you will face challenges that exceed what would be expected from a normal trainee, on a different programme. The good news is that this prepares you for anything. You'll develop compassion, understanding and a real sense of responsibility for your students. You'll learn how important the role of a teacher truly is in improving the lives of young people, and that equality is a cause worth fighting for.

Teach First Eligibility

In order to join Teach First, you will have to make sure that you meet their eligibility criteria. You'll need to have passed the Professional Skills Test before applying, and as you can imagine, given the difficulty of the role, there are a number of set qualification expectations. We've listed the educational requirements below:

Early Years Teaching and Primary Applicants

In order to qualify for Early Years teaching, you will need a degree of 2:1 or higher in one of the following, or an A*, A or B grade A-level in two of them:

Early Childhood Studies	Psychology	Art and Design
History	Maths	Geography
Music	P.E	R.E
Foreign Languages	ICT	Science
English	Design and Technology	

Secondary Applicants

In order to qualify for Secondary teaching, you will need a degree of 2:1 or higher in one of the following subjects. Alternatively, you may have an A*, A or B grade A-level in any of subjects marked with an asterisk. In order to teach Science, you'll need at least two relevant A-levels.

Business Studies	English*	Geography
Maths*	ICT	History
Music	Science*	Religious Education
Design and Technology*	Welsh	Foreign Languages

Applying for Teach First

In order to join Teach First, you'll have to apply directly through their website. Below we have included some information on what you can expect from the application form, and the pre-application questionnaire.

Pre Application Questionnaire

The Teach First pre-application questionnaire is a short yes/no test, which assesses you based on how well you meet the Teach First values, ethos and eligibility. The questions are very simple to answer, but play an important role in deciding whether you are suitable to apply.

When going through the questionnaire, make sure you read each question carefully. The questionnaire should tell you a lot about the main aims of the organisation and whether you are the right type of person to apply. Make sure you answer each question honestly. The questionnaire is for your benefit too.

You might see questions similar to the following:

Here at Teach First, we are committed to the cause of equality in education. We should not live in a country where children are limited by their background or income. Every child deserves the right to a good education. This is something we can change. Answer yes if you are committed to helping us making this change.

Yes/No

Alternatively, you might see questions such as:

Your application form will ask you to state whether you would prefer to teach at a secondary or primary school, or in early years teaching. If you are successful in application, you'll be offered an area which is in line with your qualifications and the current needs of Teach First schools. Candidates are unable to apply directly for a particular subject or level. Having read this, please confirm that you are happy to continue.

Yes/No

Or

We have designed our recruitment process to ensure that we select candidates who can have a positive impact in our partnership schools. All candidates for Teach First must be able to demonstrate the Teach First core competencies. Please take a look at the following list, and answer yes if you feel that you can adequately demonstrate all of these qualities:

Knowledge	Leadership	Organisation	Problem Solving
Resilience	Personal Evaluation	Empathy	Interaction Skills

Yes/No

Teach First Application Form

Once you've completed the pre-application questionnaire, you will move onto the application form itself. First you'll need to provide an email address (make sure you use something sensible) and sign a data protection agreement.

<u>Here is what you can generally expect to see in the application form:</u>

- **Personal Details**

Full Name:

DOB:

Mobile Contact Number:

Current Location:

- **Undergraduate Study Information**

University:

Degree Type:

Degree Category:

Year of Completion:

End Result:

University Region:

Country of University:

- **Teach First Partnerships and Other Schemes**

Teach First has a number of different partnerships, with different organisations. The reason for this is that Teach

First helps candidates to develop transferable skills, which they can take from the classroom into other areas of expertise. In this section of the application form, you'll be asked whether you would be interested in taking part in any other schemes or programmes, in conjunction with Teach First.

- **Your Interests**

In this section, you'll be given a list of choices based on your interests and reasons for joining the programme. The reason for this is so that Teach First can better ascertain your motivations and personality. The list might look something similar to this:

- I am mainly interested in the Teach First ethos, and want to pursue a career in teaching.

- I am mainly interested in pursuing a career in teaching.

- I am mainly interested in developing my personal skills and the corporate opportunities that might arise from completing Teach First.

- I am mainly interested in the financial rewards of Teach First.

- I am mainly interested in the ethos of Teach First, and would love the chance to develop my skills.

- I am mainly interested in the corporate connections associated with Teach First, and the prestige of the programme.

• <u>Education</u>

Next, you'll be given a section enquiring about your marks and qualifications. This should be fairly easy to complete. First, you'll be asked to confirm that you attended a school in the UK, before filling in information on the details of this school. You can do this for both primary and secondary school.

Then, the form will provide you with a list of subjects, and you'll be asked something along the lines of:

Please tick all of the subjects in which you have an A*, A or B grade at A-level.

Are you able to speak fluent Welsh?

• <u>Equal Opportunities</u>

Finally, you'll need to fill in an equal opportunities form.

Once your application has been processed, it will be reviewed and looked over by two members of the Teach First recruitment team. Then, if you are successful, you will be invited to attend an Assessment Centre. At the assessment centre, you will take part in the following exercises:

Teaching a pre-prepared seven minute lesson. You'll need to demonstrate your subject knowledge to the class, and show your communication skills. Once this exercise is over, you'll need to make a structured self-evaluation of your own performance. Later in this guide, we've provided you with a sample lesson planning kit, to help you out with this!

Case study. This will consist of a group exercise, and then a one-to-one chat with an assessor. The assessor and yourself will evaluate your individual performance, and that of the group as a whole. The key traits to passing this exercise are honesty, teamwork and communication.

Competency-based interview. Finally, you'll be given a competency based interview with an assessor. We've got a full interview section later in this guide, to help you cement your place on the programme. We fully encourage you to use this resource when preparing for your assessment centre.

Top Teaching Tips!

Study groups are great. You should do your utmost to help your students form these groups, allocate responsibility within the group and decide on what work will be done. Peer-to-peer learning is one of the most important educatory tools available.

Chapter 6
Other Training Routes

In this chapter, we'll be taking a look at the 2 final training routes available to teachers. These are:

• The Assessment Only Route

• Researchers In Schools

Combined with the previous chapters, the information provided here should give you a solid overview of which route is best for you.

The Assessment Only Route

The Assessment Only route allows experienced teachers who don't yet have QTS, to demonstrate that they meet the QTS standards, without them needing to take part in any further training. By the end of this route, you will have proved that you meet the Teachers' Standards, laid out by the National College for Teaching and Leadership.

In order to pass, you will need to provide detailed evidence that confirms you meet these standards. In order to do this, you will be assessed by an AO provider in your current place of work, and you'll also need to have passed the Professional Skills Test before being accepted. The assessors will judge you based on the lessons that they observe, and will measure your performance in these lessons against the teacher core competencies and expectations.

To qualify for the Assessment Only route, you must be an unqualified teacher, who has taught in at least 2 schools, either in an early years or further education setting.

There are a wide number of universities, schools and colleges that offer the Assessment Only route. In order to undergo the assessment, it will cost a fee of £2,675 plus VAT, and a non-refundable deposit of £200.

What are the Benefits?

There are a number of benefits to Assessment Only which separate it from other training routes.

Firstly, there is the timescale. As you might have guessed, the Assessment Only route is one of the quickest (if not the quickest) available, since you won't have to go through a period of extensive training. You'll already have completed the required training, through working in a school, so you will essentially skip this part of the process. The extensiveness of the assessment process will come down to the location in which you are teaching, and your own qualities as an educator. This all means that you will become a qualified teacher in no time at all!

Secondly, since you will already be earning a wage, this will mean you can move up the teacher pay scale once you've passed the assessment stage. Again, this will depend largely on the institution in which you are teaching. You'll also be able to work in maintained/state schools.

Assessment Only Eligibility

The eligibility requirements for Assessment Only will depend largely on the provider.

However, there are some basic requirements:

General requirements:

- You must hold a UK first degree, or equivalent.

- You must have a Grade C or equivalent in GCSE English and Maths. In order to teach pupils aged 3-11, you must also have a Grade C or equivalent in a Science-based subject.

- You must have taken a full DBS Check through your current school, and must be able to provide the date and number of this check.

- You must have met the general state requirements for healthy and physical capacity to teach.

Suitability requirements:

You must be able to demonstrate that you have taught in at least one of the following settings, for at least 120 days, in at least 2 different schools:

- A state school.

- A state-maintained special school.

- A City Technology College.

- A City College for the Technology of the Arts.

- An Academy.

- An independent school.

- A further education institution.

You must also be able to show that you can meet the Teacher Standard's, across at least 2 consecutive age ranges. These ranges are as follows:

- 3 to 5 years old. *(This is known as the Early Years foundation bracket.)*

- 5 to 7 years old. *(This is known as Year 1 and 2.)*

- 7 to 9 years old. *(This is known as Year 3 and 4.)*

- 9 to 11 years old. *(This is known as Year 5 and 6.)*

- 11 to 14 years old. *(This is known as Year 7, Year 8 and Year 9.)*

- 14 to 16 years old. *(This is known as Year 10 and 11.)*

- 16 to 19 years old. *(This is known as Year 12 and 13.)*

<u>In order to take the Assessment Only route, it's also imperative that:</u>

- You have the full support of the school in which you are working. The reason for this is that the school itself will need to be heavily involved in the process. You'll be teaching in their institution, and therefore it's essential that the environment is suitable for assessment. Furthermore, the school will need to provide mentor support. Before you start the assessment, your school will need to sign an agreement form to demonstrate their backing.

- You must have passed the NCTL QTS Skills Tests, in

Numeracy and Literacy.

- You must have a subject knowledge which is at the expected level of the required Teachers Standards.

- You must be able to demonstrate the teacher core competencies.

- You must be able to read, write and communicate to a high standard in the English language.

Applying for Assessment Only

In order to apply for the Assessment Only route, you will need to apply directly through a provider. Below we have given you a full list of accredited providers for this route, along with a telephone number for each provider. Please note that these contact numbers are subject to change. This is not an extensive list and interested candidates should see https://getintoteaching.education.gov.uk for more information. To make things easier, we've broken the schools down according to the region that they are in.

*See **Appendix A** for a list of accredited providers for the Assessment Only route.*

Assessment Only Application Form

In order to apply for the Assessment Only route, you will need to complete the online application form. This is a hugely extensive form, which requires both the signature of the candidate and the school in which you are working.

Below we've included the type of things that you should expect to see in your application form:

SAMPLE APPLICATION FORM

PART A
Personal Details

Title	Dr Mr Mrs Miss Ms

First name

Surname

Previous Surname

Address

Postcode

Daytime telephone number

Evening Telephone Number

Mobile number

Email address

Gender   Male   Female

Nationality

Date of birth

National Insurance Number

Do you have any special needs? Specify below.

Education

Name and address of establisment	Started	Finished	Full/part time

GCSEs (or equivalent)	Grade	Date achieved
English and Maths		
Science (Primary School only)		

A-levels	Grade	Date achieved

Higher education

Title of degree

Country of study

Awarded by

Main subjects

Subsidiary subjects

Date studied from

Date completed

Previous applications to QTS

Has the applicant failed or withdrawn from a QTS assessment in the past?   Yes   No

If yes, give details including course title and provider.

Is there documentation as to why you failed or withdrew from the process? Attach to your application.

Teacher Experience

School/college

Type of school   Middle   Secondary   Academy
Higher Ed   Specialist   Other

Country

Dates of teacher experience

What Key Stage did you gain your work experience?

What year did you gain work experience in?

Specify the number of pupils in the class.

Was you in charge of the whole class?

Hours per week.

Subject areas and topics you taught.

Personal statement

Why should you be offered a place?

PART B

Information about the school

School applied to
Name of school:
Address:
Telephone number:
Email address:
Will the school be the employer?
Is the school in an OFSTED category? Please specify.

Type of school.

Is the school already involved in this training route?

Subject area and students

School/college

Dates of teacher experience

What Key Stage did you gain your work experience?

What year did you gain work experience in?

Specify the number of pupils in the class.

Were you in charge of the whole class?

Hours per week.

Subject areas and topics you taught.

Progress

Progress of applicant

Who is responsible for the applicant?

Name:

Address:

Contact information:

What is the experience of the person who is in charge of the aforementioned applicant?

How is the applicant going to be monitored during their position at this establishment?

PART C

References

References (to be filled out by your current Head teacher or principal)

Name of applicant:

Name of referee:

School/college:

Address:

Telephone number:

Email address:

Give your views on whether the aforementioned applicant is able and ready.

Please indicate any other comments you wish to offer regarding the application of the aforementioned.

PART D

Declaration

Both the applicant and the school will need to read the terms and conditions, and sign the declaration form that completed the application form.

Make sure that you read the terms carefully to ensure that you meet each statement.

SIGNED

PRINT

DATE

Researchers in Schools (RIS)

Researchers in Schools (RIS) is a training and development programme, which is exclusive to researchers who have achieved a doctorate. The aim of the programme is to train these researchers to become fantastic teachers, and subject leaders in the educatory field. They provide their candidates with the time and financial backing to carry out their research, publications and attend subject related conferences.

Researchers in Schools takes high calibre applicants, specifically focusing on communication and research ability, and then trains them to work as teachers in non-selective maintained schools. They do so through their own Initial Teaching Training Programme, or ITTP.

The programme itself is delivered through a combination of classroom-based teaching and research. Candidates will start off the programme by taking a summer training module, where they will be taught essential elements of teaching practice, theory and other communication-based skills. Following this module, you will be placed in a school, where you will practice on the job and work towards QTS. RIS candidates will be paid an extensive salary whilst taking the programme. You should contact the course providers for more information on this.

What Makes Reasearchers in Schools so Unique?

So, why should you choose RIS above another training

route? Apart from the fact that the course is limited to candidates with a doctorate, there are a number of aims that the RIS programme delivers upon:

Increasing subject knowledge. Due to the fact that RIS is training candidates with doctorates, the end result of the course is that those who do go on to become teachers will provide the schools in which they are working with a fantastic service. As a doctorate, you are already a high-level subject specialist. By learning how to teach this information to pupils, in a classroom setting, you will be greatly benefitting the school and the wider subject field. The long term effect of this is that we'll eventually have more and more subject specialists, as a result of specialist led teaching programmes such as RIS.

Encouraging research. One of the principle aims of RIS is to utilise the research skills of their high quality candidates. These skills will then be passed onto pupils in the classroom setting; meaning that the educational sector and the pupils within it are being given better tools to help them focus their own enquiries, and conduct research.

Better prepared pupils. The candidates on RIS will either be completing their doctorate or have recently finished. As a result, they are fantastically placed to teach pupils about the challenges ahead, prepare them for their own research and encourage university as the next step.

RIS Structure

Researchers in Schools is a bespoke training route, specifically for PhD graduates. The aim of the programme is to use the academic expertise offered by these candidates, to benefit pupils in schools and universities.

The programme is 2 years in length. In the first year, you'll achieve QTS, and in the second year you will complete your NQT. This will be done through a combination of training, teaching and mentoring. You will also receive ongoing CPD training throughout the 2 years, and will take on a number of research-based projects, which aim to support pupils.

Following the completion of the 2 years, candidates will also have an option to take a third year. Completion of this year will mean that candidates are eligible for the Research Leader in Education Award. This is a professional qualification, which furthers educational research skills and gives you more tools for applying them in the school environment. The RLE award is extremely prestigious, and will stand out when used in a CV or job application. It shows dedication and commitment.

Researchers in Schools is a salaried programme. This means that you will be employed by your host school during the training period. You'll receive a salary throughout the training year, but won't be teaching a full timetable until you reach the second year of the programme. One of the biggest benefits of RIS is that the salary offered is generally amongst the largest among different training routes, and all of your training fees are covered. Once you've received the second year of the programme, as an NQT, you'll move up to the main pay scale of the school, and will receive a £1000 bursary; designed to help with academic research and further credits.

Below we've broken this down into more detail, so that you can see exactly what you'll be doing in each year of the programme.

Year 1

In Year 1, you will work towards gaining Qualified Teacher Status. You will attend teacher training once per week, and will work in a school for another 3 days of the week. Your final day will be spent researching and working towards the RIS aims and ambitions.

The Year 1 training will be delivered by expert professionals in the field. You'll take part in evidence-based teaching, research, observation and personal reflection. All of this will help you to develop independent teaching skills, and perfect your practice.

Year 2

Now that you are an NQT, you will work towards completing an NQT year in a placement school. You'll spend approximately 16 hours (4 days a week), teaching in this school. Furthermore, you will move on to the main pay scale for teachers.

Your placement will see you working with the same pupils that you taught in Year 1, to build familiarity. On the one day that you aren't teaching, you will be taking part in research-based activities, with the aim of supporting pupils.

Along with all of this, candidates will continue to receive professional development training, such as teaching theory and educational research.

Year 3

This is an optional year, however it is compulsory if you are teaching Maths or Physics. If you do choose to take this year, you will continue teaching and the Research Leader in Education Award programme will open up for you. This will help you to further develop your research skills and use these in the school environment.

Applying for RIS

In order to apply for RIS, you'll need to complete the RIS online application form. This is an extremely important form, so you need to make sure that you complete it to the best of your ability. The form will provide you with the opportunity to demonstrate your academic experience, and why this makes you the right fit for the course.

At the end of the form, you will be given 8 different questions to answer.

These questions are based around the following:

Questions 1-3. These are questions based around your motivations for becoming a teacher. You will need to demonstrate that you have a good understanding of the aims of the RIS programme, and how you personally intend to achieve these. In your answers, you should use your own experiences of teaching, school and education as a platform for your answer. You need to demonstrate an enthusiasm for the cause, and that you have considered the type of challenges you'll face on the course.

Questions 4-8. The second set of questions will be based around the teaching core competencies. You'll be asked to demonstrate occasions or examples of when you have used the core competencies of teaching. In the interview section of this guide, we've included a full breakdown on how to answer these types of questions.

The RIS also allows you to attach your CV to the application form. This is a fantastic opportunity to further boost your chances of success. Let's look at how to complete this in more detail:

CV and Cover Letter

A CV and Cover Letter go hand-in-hand, to increase your chances of gaining a job position, or in this case a position on the RIS course. Much like an application form, the two documents should tell the course providers about your personal qualities, qualifications and experience.

You should start by constructing a cover letter:

Cover Letter

A cover letter serves as a written introduction to your CV, and helps the providers get to know you on a more personal level. In your cover letter you should include your skills and interests, a bit of information on your background and why you are applying for Researchers in Schools. Make sure you tailor your letter to the providers specifically. Mention the value of research, your PHD and why you want to teach.

Now, write up your own cover letter in the box provided. Compare it with the example cover letter below:

Sample Cover Letter

'You should endeavour to find out the name of whoever will be receiving your letter and address it to them personally, using their full title.)

I am writing to apply for a place on the Researchers in Schools teacher training programme.

I am an enthusiastic, driven and hard-working PHD student, with a passion for making a difference in the lives of others. I believe that teaching is the perfect route for me, and see Researchers in Schools as the premier programme for me to train in.

As an English PHD student, I am extremely familiar with the concepts that are central to this course, and I believe that I share the same ethos as RIS. I am someone who strongly believes in the value of teaching pupils how to utilise the resources at their disposal, and I feel that we should be doing everything that we can to encourage students to develop their research skills. I consider myself to be a specialist in English Literature, and therefore I know I can bring an extremely high level of expertise to this programme, and to the schools in which I will be working.

Furthermore, as a university student, I share the same goal as RIS in promoting university to school pupils. I am someone who cares deeply about the education system and reducing inequality/promoting equal opportunities within it. Not only do we need to reduce inequality, but we also need to teach pupils that education does not have to stop with school. They can go on and make a success of themselves at university and other esteemed institutions. With the backing of RIS, I know that I am the right person to promote this message.

Thank you for taking the time to read my application, I sincerely hope that you will consider me for a place on this course.

Yours faithfully,

As you can see, in the above cover letter we have presented ourselves as a candidate who is a great fit for the course. If you can link your own experience and skills with the RIS aims and ethos, you will really increase your chances of gaining a place on the course.

RIS CV

Of course, no cover letter is complete without a CV. Generally, when you are submitting your CV, you should keep it to a length of 2 pages maximum. Below we have included a sample CV, to give you a better idea of how to layout your own. In our example CV, we have elaborated in more detail during the 'work experience' section. This is to give you a good idea of the various types of experience you might choose to include, how you can use this experience to benefit your application and how you can present it to RIS. When you write your own application, try to trim the information down, so that you have only used information that is relevant to the course itself.

<u>Example CV</u>

Madeline Humphrey

Smith Street

Smith Town

Smithshire

Tel: 01634 123456

Email: MaddieHumphrey@emailaddresshere.com

Personal profile:

I am a driven, enthusiastic and hard-working individual, who has just completed a PHD in English Literature. I am extremely proud to have a doctorate to my name, and I now want to use this as a platform for career success. I consider myself to be a caring person, who possesses great leadership skills; and I place huge value on the education system. For this reason, I believe that teaching would be perfect for me.

The Researchers in Schools programme is hugely impressive to me. I believe that your organisation's aims are fully in line with my own ethos, values and skillset. I am in a strong position to promote both research and university access to pupils in schools; having benefitted hugely from both during my education. As a subject specialist in English, I believe that I am the right person to deliver a fantastic quality of education to the pupils in your partnership schools.

Academic experience:

Smith School:

GCSE Psychology: A

GCSE Maths: B

GCSE English: A

GCSE History: B

GCSE Geography: A

AS Level English Literature: A

AS Level Psychology: A

A-Level English Literature: A

A-Level Psychology: A

Smith University:

BA English and American Literature, 2:1

MA English Literature: Distinction

PHD English Literature: Pass

Previous employment history, dates and duties:

PHD in English Literature. 14/09/2013-14/07/2016

This course was funded by my university, and involved conducting large amounts of independent research, with the goal of completing a 50,000 word thesis. The thesis title was *Dickens and Other 19th Century Works*. Throughout my PHD, I spent large amounts of time leading workshop groups and seminars, and completed two observation periods in local schools. I gained leadership skills and experience and learned the importance of using external resources in my work, and organisation.

12/07/2013-12/08/2013: 1 month of work experience assisting at Smith day-care/nursery.

This position involved working with those in charge, as part of a team, to ensure the wellbeing and safety of young attendees. Activities included: creating a fun and friendly atmosphere for the children, participating in group singing exercises and helping to put children down for naps. This position also involved communicating with parents who were dropping off/collecting or assisting with the playgroup activities.

14/10/2013-24/10/2013: 2 weeks of work experience assisting student services at Smith elementary school.

This position involved working with student services to provide a support base for children under the age of 11. The initial week was spent shadowing those in charge, before assisting in the second week. Activities included: meeting in a team setting with students to rectify their behaviour, meeting students one to one to discuss behavioural changes, and submitting reviews/ reports on particular students. The position required me to understand and apply large amounts of behavioural theory

10/10/2011-15/12/2011: 2 month placement at How2Help.

This position involved working in a voluntary organisation, dealing with troubled service users. The work was emotionally challenging and I encountered a wide range of issues, including alcoholism and drug abuse. I was required to apply large amounts of behavioural and interventional theory, in order to assist the users involved. For a small part of this placement, I also worked in the How2Help charity shop.

Core competencies:

I am a highly experienced and capable researcher, who is just as able to promote the value in researching as conducting research myself.

I am a highly relatable, compassionate and empathetic person with the ability to bond with young people, and lead by example.

I have fantastic communicational abilities, as well as good organisational skills.

I have a good level of experience in dealing with vulnerable people, particularly children.

I have a great working knowledge of behavioural theory, concepts and framework.

Significant achievements:

Recently completed my PHD in English Literature, and before that a Masters in English Literature.

Built up great relationships with students in school based placements.

Have developed leadership skills which can be carried over to the classroom environment.

Successfully reviewed and implemented detailed changes to the behavioural plans of students in a school; with great results.

Hobbies and interests:

When I am not working, I spend most of my time socialising with friends and family. I love to keep fit, and was a member of various sports teams at both school and university. I'm also someone who is really interested in animal wellbeing, and I take great value in promoting this aim.

Now, let's look at the application form in more detail. Along with the standard personal details sections of the form, and education sections, you'll also be given sections such as the below.

Researchers In Schools Application Form

Educational Background:

Q1. Do you have a C grade or higher, in Maths and English at GCSE level or equivalent?

Q2. Candidates who do not have grades of at least a C in Maths or English at GCSE level, will need to take responsibility for sitting and passing tests that are equivalent to these. An offer from RIS will be conditioned on passing these examinations. Please tick yes if you are happy with this.

Q3. Applicants for RIS must have completed their doctorate at a registered higher education institution, by *date of year of application*. Please tick yes if you are happy with this.

Q4. Please confirm that you are fully available to work, full-time, from *date of start of course* and then continuously throughout the course.

Q5. Candidates for RIS must complete their Professional Skills Tests by *date of start of course*, if offered a place on the course. Please tick yes if you are happy with this.

Q6. Please confirm that you do not already hold QTS in the UK.

Teaching Preferences:

Q1. Using the four boxes provided, select which subject you would prefer to train in as a teacher. You should allocate your preferences according to the subject you would like to teach most. For example, if your preferred choice is English, this should go in box 1 (first preference).

Q2. Now, please select the region in which you would prefer to complete your training. You should allocate your preferences according to the region you would like to teach most. For example, if your preferred region, this should go in box 1 (first preference).

Please note: *When you select your region, you are selecting the region in which you would like your placement school to be based. Unfortunately RIS cannot guarantee candidates a place in their exact chosen school or region. Your placement school could be placed anywhere within this region.*

Q3. Can you think of any circumstances which might hinder your ability to relocate, should you be successful in application?

Q4. Are you currently in the process, or have you ever been, of applying to train as a teacher via another training route than RIS?

Q5. Have you already completed your Professional Skills Test?

RIS Application Form Questions

During this section, you will be asked a number of different questions, based around your motivations for applying to RIS, your desire to teach and your understanding of the programme and its goals.

In our interview section, we've provided you with a wide range of responses, which can be used to craft your own answers to these questions. However, applying to RIS is different to other training routes. Candidates for this route need to have a sustained interest and passion for using research. Therefore, your answers need to reflect this. Let's have a look at a typical question from the application form, and how to respond to it:

Q. The aim of Researchers in Schools is to increase overall subject expertise. The programme does this by promoting sustained research, and promoting university access to non-selective state schools. In 300 words or less, tell us why this programme appeals to you and what you could bring to the course?

Sample response

There are a number of reasons that RIS appeals to me. Firstly, as a PHD graduate, I am hugely excited to put my research skills to great use. I am someone who has spent many years in the education system, and this means that I have fine-tuned my research skills to an exceptional level. I could not have successfully completed my PHD without this, and this is why I believe it is essential that we teach pupils how to utilise and make the most of the resources and tools available to them, as early as possible. By encouraging in-depth research, we stand a better chance of creating a more intelligent, engaged and well-informed generation of graduates.

Secondly, I am passionate about promoting university access to all pupils. Education is for everybody, it shouldn't depend on your income or the quality of your schooling. I want to make pupils see that there is a value in studying after their school years; that they can go on to make something of themselves in the field and the RIS programme will help me to do this.

Finally, I am hugely impressed by what I see as an outstanding course. I have conducted thorough research into RIS before applying; including speaking to current participants and trainee teachers, and I firmly believe this is the right way forward for me. I have the passion, enthusiasm and drive to succeed on your course, and the research fundamentals needed to back this up. I believe I'd be an excellent fit, and I hope you'll consider my application.

<u>You might also be asked questions such as:</u>

- Tell us why you have decided to become a teacher.

- What is it that makes you so passionate about working with young people?

- Identify 4 challenges that you expect to face on this course, and how you will deal with them.

- Describe a time when you have demonstrated leadership, either inside or outside of the classroom.

Next Steps

Once you've completed and sent off the application form, you will be invited to attend an Assessment Centre. This will take place at one of the RIS partner schools, and will be split up into a number of different activities. The assessment day will consist of:

- Delivering a mini-lesson.

- Completing a self-evaluation form based on the mini-lesson.

- Taking part in a group exercise.

- Having a one-to-one interview.

If the thought of delivering a mini-lesson scares you, then don't worry! Below we've included some basic lesson planning forms, and a lesson plan checklist to help you plan for your exercise!

Later in this guide, we've included detailed advice on how to conduct yourself during the interview.

LESSON PLANNING

SUBJECT	LEVEL	TUTOR	DATE	DURATION

OUTCOMES AND OBJECTIVES

1.

2.

3.

4.

RESOURCES REQUIRED:

_____

_____

_____

_____

_____

_____

_____

ASSESSMENTS BEING USED:

Quizzes or exams _____

Self-assessments_____

Group exercises_____

Peer-assessments_____

Coursework_____

FEEDBACK ON ACTIVITIES:

WRITTEN   ORAL   GROUP   ONE-TO-ONE

BREAKDOWN OF LESSON:

INTRODUCTION:

LEARNING OBJECTIVES:

ACTIVITIES:

1.

2.

3.

EXTENSION ACTIVITIES:

DISCUSSION OF WHAT IS LEARNT:

ADDITIONAL SUPPORT DURING THE LESSON:

EVALUATE TEACHING PERFORMANCE

What went well?

How well did the students interact with the lesson?

What areas do you need to work on?

Is there anything that needs to be recovered in the next lesson?

Did your students understand everything being taught?

How can you adapt your teaching style if students didn't respond well to the lesson?

Was the lesson set to a high enough standard?

Top Teaching Tips!

After every writing activity, ask your students to compare and contrast their responses. This will go to show that there is more than one way of thinking about the topic, and encourages students to think independently!

Chapter 7
Journal of a Trainee Teacher

Now that we've provided you with a breakdown of how to apply, what modules you'll take and how you'll be assessed, it's time to look at what a trainee teacher actually gets up to.

We've asked Mark, a PGCE student, to give us a breakdown of his PGCE course. In the past year, Mark completed his training to teach English in a secondary school.

We've already shown you what kind of modules you'll be studying, so we're going to jump straight ahead to Mark's second school placement!

If you are taking SCITT or Schools Direct, pay close attention. Many of the scenarios listed here should give you a fantastic insight into what you'll experience when teaching in schools.

Weeks 1-2

Mark arrives back at University in January excited for the next 5 months of his life. He has already conducted a period of observation in a local school during November, and now he is ready to develop his skills in a second placement. The first thing that Mark has to complete is an essay-based assignment, comparing 2 different teaching theories and how they impact teachers in the classroom environment.

Once Mark's essay has been handed in, it's time to start preparing for the 2nd placement. Mark is in a different, albeit closer school this time, within the local area. In order to prepare the candidates for the challenges ahead, Mark and his coursemates have several days where they practice the following:

Mock interviews. These are an important part of the PGCE. Course providers are looking for a high success rate from candidates that they train, and part of this is training candidates to pass teaching interviews. *(See Interview chapter for further details).*

Presentations. These will generally be on topics such as your personal development, learning theory and other professional study based topics. You can expect to deliver a wide variety of presentations during your time on the PGCE. This is great practice for when you are standing up in front of a class delivering information.

Meeting their school mentors. Throughout your time on the PGCE, and especially during your placements, you'll be in constant contact with an assigned school mentor. Course providers and schools understand how difficult and stressful life can be for trainee teachers, and therefore it's important to have someone there whom you can talk to. This is not just for your benefit either. Your mentors will play a crucial role in your final assessment mark. It's important for schools to make sure that they aren't putting someone in front of a class who isn't ready or is unprepared to teach. This would hurt their reputation as a school and damage their students' marks.

Behaviour management. This is something that you'll spend a lot of time working on during the PGCE, and is an essential element of being a teacher. Another word for behaviour management is 'discipline'. The core concept that you'll be taught on the PGCE is that bad behaviour is very often not something that the individual/child in question is in control of. As a teacher, it is your job to understand that every pupil is different, and to show your students how to identify behavioural boundaries. In the same way, PGCE course providers understand that all teachers are different, and that different personalities command different levels of respect in the classroom. This is part of the reason that you need to make the most of your observation periods. You'll pick up essential tips and tricks from experienced professionals in this way, and learn how to start controlling your classes.

<u>Weeks 3-4</u>

Mark begins week 3 at his new school/placement. After 2 days of observation, he is asked to deliver a full English lesson to a class of Year 7 pupils. Unfortunately, Mark's initial lesson does not go to plan. The pupils are badly behaved, and midway through the lesson Mark has to send one of them out for throwing a rubber at his head. After the lesson, Mark sits down with the teacher whose class it was, to discuss how things went. Mark admits that he is surprised by how immature the Year 7 pupils are, after spending an observation period working with Year 6 students in a primary school. The teacher reassures Mark that he did the right thing by sending the student out, and offers some pointers for the next lesson. Unfortunately for Mark, OFSTED will be observing the school in the next 3 days, and therefore he won't be allowed to teach until the following week.

Week 4 begins with good news. The school passed their OFSTED report with flying colours, and now Mark will be able to teach again. He starts off on Monday with the same class that he taught during the previous week. Before the lesson starts off, Mark has a serious chat with the class about their behaviour. This seems to have a calming effect, as the class are much better behaved and the lesson goes extremely well. After the lesson, his tutor congratulates Mark on the turnaround.

Mark teaches one further lesson on Monday, which is to a Year 8 English group. Learning from last time, Mark comes into the lesson taking a strict approach from the get-go. This leads to a lesson which runs smoothly, but part of the feedback that Mark receives after the lesson (from the teacher) is that the class weren't fully engaged with his material.

Unfortunately, Mark spends Tuesday, Wednesday and Thursday off sick. He has quickly realised a big lesson; schools are full of germs which can spread quickly in the close quarter environment. Upon returning to school, Mark has a Friday progress meeting with his mentor, before taking the same two classes again during the day. This time, Mark manages to engage with and keep the second class interested. He receives positive feedback from his tutor, and has just completed his first two weeks teaching in a school.

<u>Weeks 5-6</u>

Now that Mark has reached week 5, things have stepped up a gear. Mark will be taking over the teaching for both of the previously mentioned classes, and will also be teaching 2 other classes. This means that he'll frequently be teaching lessons in a row, and will have a great deal of lesson planning to do. Mark will also face the task of getting up to speed with different schemes of work, whilst at the same time writing out a crucial course assignment essay. During his previous meeting with his mentor, Mark discussed a number of organisational strategies, which he is intending to incorporate this week.

On Tuesday of week 5, Mark teaches 4 lessons in a row. This leaves him emotionally drained; and he still has to go home and plan for the next 2 days. Along with this, Mark also faces the prospect of applying for future placements in different schools. Positions are starting to open up, and this means that candidates are fully encouraged to apply, both to start earning a proper wage once their PGCE is over, and at the very least to gain some real experience of interviewing.

Week 6 is a difficult week for Mark. He realises that the more his classes get to know him, the less respect they have for him. Mark is also struggling with ideas for keeping his lessons fresh and exciting. His Year 7 group have begun misbehaving again, and on Wednesday he has to have another serious chat with the group before the lesson starts. When two of the students are unrepentant, Mark removes them from the room and sends them to the head's office. Thankfully, this seems to have a positive impact on the rest of the group who behave well for the remainder of the lesson. Mark's Year 9 poetry group are also misbehaving. His attempts to have a serious chat with the entire group fall flat, and do not improve things. During their debrief session, Mark's tutor encourages him to have a one-to-one discussion with the main perpetrators before the next lesson.

Weeks 7-8

Mark spends the next week in between school and university. He has now been set another two important assignments, and is struggling to keep on top of things. He is having difficulty with the early morning starts in particular. Mark's tutor assures him that this is completely normal and that most PGCE candidates struggle with this element at first. Fortunately, week 7 sees a turnaround for Mark in the behaviour of his classes. After taking his tutor's advice, Mark's attempt to amend the behaviour of his Year 9 poetry class pays off; and the group surprises Mark by producing outstanding homework. This makes Mark realise that he has been pitching the level of his lessons a little too low, and that perhaps this is why the class haven't been engaged with the material. His tutor agrees with this, and recommends that he ups the difficulty during the next session.

Mark is also teaching a Year 10 class this week, and he is surprised by what he finds. Having expected the group to take to the subject, Shakespeare, with ease; Mark is disappointed to discover that at least half of the group don't have a clue what is written in the plays and can't translate from the book directly. He comes away from this lesson having learnt that knowledge does not necessarily change with age; every class still has a wide variety of learning levels, and that he will need to plan a whole range of different tasks to accommodate this.

Week 8 is extremely different for Mark, in that he is being

interviewed for 2 teaching positions. The first position is in a girl's grammar school. The biggest benefit of this school, in Mark's view, is that it is an extremely reputable institution where the staff are known to offer fantastic support to trainees. The downside is that the school is half an hour away from his house. Upon arriving at the school and being given some key information about the school ethos, Mark is asked to wait for a while before being interviewed. Mark struggles initially with the interview but quickly is able to use the skills taught by his course providers to turn things around. Following the interview, candidates are taken to meet their potential future colleagues from the English department, and taken around the school. At the end of the day, Mark is offered a position as a trainee teacher in the department! He is given a deadline of 3 days' time to respond.

The next day, Mark heads off for his second interview. This time, the interview will be held at a mixed school. While this school is not a grammar school, the location is only 10 minutes from his house. Furthermore, Mark likes the fact that the school is less exam-driven. For him, this indicates less pressure, and allows him to focus on getting to know the students better. The only downside of this is that Mark will have to deal with more challenging students, who will present issues unlike anything Mark has faced before in his 2 previous schools. Mark feels that behavioural management is the weakest element of his skillset at the moment, and therefore this could be a problem. From the moment that Mark arrives at the school, however, he feels right at home. The staff are extremely friendly, and the interview goes really well.

Two days later, Mark is called back for another interview where he meets the head teacher, who offers him the job right there and then. Delighted, Mark accepts. He will be starting straight after the completion of his PGCE!

<u>Weeks 9-10</u>

Week 9 once again consists of a change of scenery for Mark. He will be spending this week teaching in a different placement, before returning to his previous school (for a final week) in week 10. During this week, Mark is teaching A-level students. This is quite a relief to Mark, who feels more at home teaching advanced subject material, similar to that which he learned during his English Master's degree. Mark really enjoys being able to have a mature discussion with his students, without the need to shout or telling them to calm down. Similarly, Mark receives extremely positive feedback from his tutor on these lessons. It seems that this could be an area/age group which Mark will aim to teach in the future…

During week 10, Mark is once again back at his 2nd placement. He'll be spending 3 days teaching here, before using Thursday and Friday to complete and hand in a crucial professional values assignment. Mark uses this as an opportunity to really put into practice everything that he has learned. He finds that the 3 days pass by much easier than before. With renewed confidence from his job offer, Mark is able to control his classes much better than before. He finishes the week by receiving letters of thanks from his Year 7 class for all the work he has put in, and leaves the second placement with his head held high. He'll be starting his next placement, in a school that is 20 minutes away, on Monday!

Weeks 11-12

Week 11 starts and Mark is teaching in a new school. Now that he has significant experience, Mark is expected to transition quickly to teaching different classes. Unlike in the other placements, his tutor will be less lenient and Mark will be expected to apply behavioural management techniques and keep control of his classes. A failure to succeed in this placement will have a damaging impact on Mark's final assessment score. Mark is already counting down the weeks until he can start earning a real wage! Although Mark initially struggles a little, he quickly comes to grips with having what is almost a full timetable of English classes; consisting of Years 7, 8 and 9. Mark is fortunate on this placement in that he is taking over classes who have just been given back their school reports. He is invited to use these reports before the lessons, to ascertain which students he should focus particular attention on.

Since this is the summer term, Mark finds that students' behaviour fluctuates, often according to how good the weather is outside. However, with exam pressure off, he finds that lessons are far more relaxed for the students and this leads to better discussion and less misbehaviour in class. In particular, Mark has great fun with a Year 9 class acting out a Shakespeare play. Weeks 11 and 12 fly by, all with positive feedback from his tutor. Mark now feels as if he is truly coming to grips with life as a teacher.

<u>Weeks 13-14</u>

Mark is now close to the end of his time on the PGCE, and with the end of the school year swiftly approaching, his students' behaviour is starting to derail slightly. Mark has discovered that teaching is a rollercoaster of emotions. When a lesson goes badly, you feel terrible and fraudulent, until the next good lesson comes around and you feel like the best teacher in the world. Mark has also learned a lot about discipline during the past 2 weeks. The school in question is far stricter on their students and the teachers whom Mark is working with have shown him how to use it to good effect. Mark has realised that in order to keep control of the classroom, you must be extremely black and white about the consequences of misbehaviour. Mark has worked on his strict approach, and it now seems to be paying off, even if he doesn't enjoy being harsh to his pupils.

<u>Weeks 15-16</u>

Mark is now in the final two weeks of his PGCE. After finishing his placement at his last school, Mark spends the final week finishing and handing in a number of crucial assignments. These assignments will all be put together in 5-10 days' time, and used to determine whether Mark has done enough to earn his PGCE certificate. Fortunately, Mark passes with flying colours, and is now in a great position to start working in the job he earned way back in week 8. He is extremely confident, and ready to start his career as a qualified English teacher!

Chapter 8
The Professional Skills Test

All candidates wishing to obtain QTS will need to pass the Professional Skills Tests in Numeracy and Literacy. As a teacher, you will need to demonstrate a high level of numeracy and literary in all areas of work.

This set of standards applies to ALL teachers, not just those who teach subjects which include numerical ability, such as mathematics. It is vital that you are fully prepared for the tests, and the first stage in your preparation is to gain an understanding of what is involved during the tests.

The Professional Skills Tests are a pass or fail, with a minimum competence test standard which is based on a range of practical skills deemed important for a teacher's general professional practice. The Teaching Agency will hold a number of test forms in each subject area and you will be assigned a test paper, picked at random, when you enter the test. Because the test paper is picked at random, there is no way of determining the type of questions you will be asked. Therefore, it is vital that you prepare for every eventuality and type of question.

The test papers and questions that are held by the Teaching Agency are changed and renewed each year. All tests are piloted each year by the Teaching Agency, to ensure they are relevant to the role and of a standard that is comparable to the teaching role you will be expected to undertake. The tests themselves are taken in a secure test centre, on a computer, unless special arrangements have been granted for an alternative format.

In addition to using this guide and the test questions contained in this chapter, we also strongly recommend that you take the time to work through the bank of practice tests and support information that is made available to you on the Teaching Agency pages of the Department for Education website.

Now, let's look at each section of the test individually:

Professional Skills Numeracy Test

The QTS numeracy test is a computer based assessment, which covers 3 separate areas: mental arithmetic, interpreting and using written data, and solving written arithmetic problems. You will only have a total of 48 minutes to complete the test, unless you have specifically requested special arrangements to be made.

Audio (mental arithmetic) questions

The first part of the test is a mental arithmetic section. This comprises of an audio test, which you listen to through provided headphones. This area of the test will assess your competence in the following key areas:

• Time;

• Fractions;

• Percentages;

• Measurements;

• Conversions.

During this section, each of the questions are individually-timed and you are not allowed to use a calculator.

Written numeracy questions

During this part of the numeracy skills test you will need to answer computer-based questions. You are permitted to use a calculator during this test but not your own. An on-screen calculator will be provided. The test questions will assess your ability to interpret and use written data in the following key areas:

- Identifying trends correctly;

- Making comparisons in order to draw conclusions;

- Interpreting information accurately.

You will also be tested on your ability to solve written arithmetic problems, which are set in a variety of situations and will include:

- Time;

- Money;

- Proportion and ratio;

- Percentages, fractions and decimals;

- Measurements (e.g. distance, area);

- Conversions (e.g. from one currency to another, from fractions to decimals or percentages);

- Averages (including mean, median, mode and range where relevant);

- Using simple formulae.

The Numeracy skills test format

Each test consists of a total of 28 questions: 12 mental arithmetic and 16 on-screen. All of the questions carry one mark regardless of the number of required responses. All the numeracy tests have been calibrated statistically against a test. The pass mark for the test is currently 63 per cent but this can vary. As with any multiple set of tests, the tests are not exactly the same difficulty, but are of an equivalent standard. A test with slightly harder questions will have a slightly lower pass mark and a test with slightly easier questions will have a slightly higher pass mark. Have a go at the practice numerical paper below, to see how you get on.

PRACTICE TEST - NUMERACY

---

*Please note = these tests are not the exact types of questions you will face in your assessment. Instead they are designed to help you improve your numerical ability in preparation for the Professional Skills Test.

ARITHMETIC

Question 1

What is ¼ as a decimal?

Answer

┌─────────────────────────┐
│   │
└─────────────────────────┘

Question 2

What is ¾ as decimal?

Answer

Question 3

What is 1/5 as a percentage?

Answer

Question 4

What is 85.5 as a percentage?

Answer

Question 5

There are 25 pupils in a class. 5 pupils have been moved from the bottom group of Literacy to the top group of Literacy. What percentage of pupils have been moved up?

Answer

Question 6

A school plans a trip to Northern Ireland. The trip involves walking 16km a day for 4 days. If 8km is approximately equivalent to 5 miles, how many miles are the students walking in total?

Answer

Question 7

In a junior school there are 420 pupils. 3/5 of them receive free hot school dinners. How many of them do not receive free hot school dinners?

Answer

Question 8

In the lunch time hall, there are 150 students. 0.3 of them are boys. How many girls are there?

Answer

Question 9

A class of 40 is creating wall art for their school. 60% of them have finished their art and are waiting for the others to finish so they can piece it all together. How many pupils have finished their wall art?

Answer

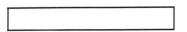

Question 10

There are 2 tiers in Year Seven Maths. 3/8 of the higher level achieved a C grade. 1/4 of the lower level also achieved a C grade. What is the total fraction (in its simplest form) for both classes combined that achieved a C grade in Maths?

Answer

Question 11

What is 60% of 580 pounds?

Answer

Question 12

A teacher gives out a Maths quiz in her GCSE Maths class. There are 29 pupils in her class. Each test takes about 6 minutes to mark, with 2 minutes to check over each test. How long in hours and minutes will it take for the teacher to finish marking the Maths quizzes?

Answer

INTERPRETING AND SOLVING MATHEMATICS

Question 1

Test marks in Maths, History and English for Year 9 are compared by three box – and – whisker diagrams shown below. Marks are shown on the vertical axis.

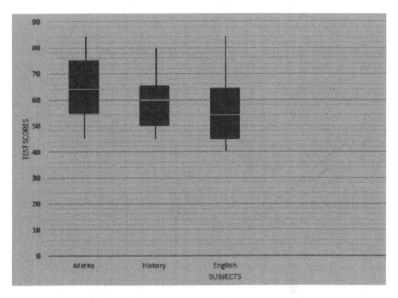

The interquartile range for Maths is higher than that for English. True or false?

The lowest mark was in History. True or false?

The median score for Maths is 65. True or false?

Question 2

Attendance for term 1 in a secondary school are compared by box-and-whisker diagrams shown below. The number of absences are shown on the vertical axis.

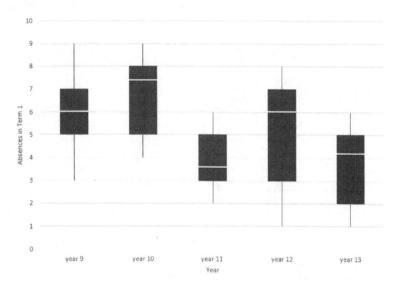

The difference between the median absences between year 9 and 12 is approximately 5. True or false?

The highest number of absences came from year 12. True or false?

The interquartile range for year 10 is higher than that of year 11. True or false?

Question 3

The set of data below shows the result in a year 9 History test for 50 pupils. The marks are out of 10. The teacher wants to find the mean mark for this test. Give your answer to 1 decimal place.

Marks in History Test	No. of pupils	No. of pupils x History Marks
1	5	1x5=5
2	1	2x1=2
3	8	
4	2	
5	7	
6	6	
7	3	
8	11	
9	4	
10	3	
Totals	50	

The mean mark is:

Question 4

A test in Science consists of three papers. The first paper is out of 70 and has weighting of 45% given to it. The second paper is out of 50 and has weighting of 40%. The third test is out of 10 and has weighting of 15%. A pupil gets 56 in the first paper, 20 in the second paper and 8 in the third paper. What is the pupil's final percentage score?

Weighted score is:

```
[                    ]
```

Question 5

A quiz in Media consists of three sections. The first section is out of 30 and has weighting of 60%. The second section is out of 20 and has a weighting of 25%. The third section is out of 10 and has weighting of 15%. A team gets 20 in the first section, 12 in the second section and 6 in the third section. What is the pupil's final percentage score?

Weighted score is:

```
[                    ]
```

Question 6

What is the difference between the total number of employees in Marketing, and the total number of employees in Sales, across the six month period?

Employees in departments of a company						
Department	January	February	March	April	May	June
Marketing	21	24	17	15	23	27
Admin	18	11	15	13	13	18
Sales	21	22	29	31	28	24
IT	19	13	17	18	22	25

Answer

Question 7

What percentage of the total number of crimes were assault-related, based on the total number of crimes?

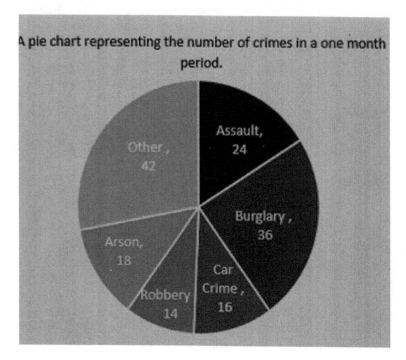

A pie chart representing the number of crimes in a one month period.

Assault, 24

Other, 42

Burglary, 36

Arson, 18

Car Crime, 16

Robbery 14

Answer

Question 8

The table below shows the sales across 6 countries for the model BMW for a 6 month period. The BMW's are imported to each country from a main dealer. Use the information provided to answer the following questions.

Country	Jan	Feb	Mar	Apr	May	June	Total
UK	21	28	15	35	31	20	150
Germany	45	48	52	36	41	40	262
France	32	36	33	28	20	31	180
Brazil	42	41	37	32	35	28	215
Spain	22	26	17	30	24	22	141
Italy	33	35	38	28	29	38	201
Total	195	214	192	189	180	179	1149

What percentage of the overall total was sold in April? To 1 decimal place.

Answer

Question 9

If the dollar amount of sales at store Q was $600,000 for 2005, what was the dollar amount of sales at the store in 2007?

STORE	PERCENT CHANGE FROM 2005 TO 2006	PERCENT CHANGE FROM 2006 TO 2007
	ANNUAL PERCENT CHANGE IN DOLLAR AMOUNT OF SALES AT FIVE RETAIL STORES FROM 2005 TO 2007	
P	-20	8
Q	-10	10
R	6	10
S	-9	-14
T	16	-6

Answer

Question 10

In England, if the petrol consumption per day dropped by 8% from 2014 to 2015, how much would the petrol consumption be in 2015?

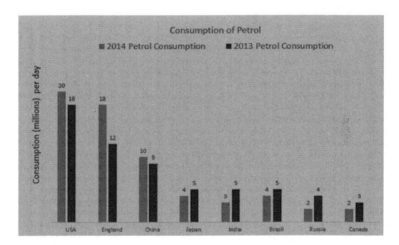

Answer

```
┌─────────────────────┐
│                     │
└─────────────────────┘
```

Question 11

The diagram below shows the plan of a building site. All angles are right angles.

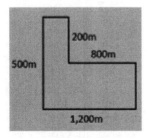

What is the area of the building site? Give your answer in hectares. 1 hectare = 10,000m² = 2.47 acres.

Answer

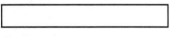

Question 12

The Siberian tiger population in Country A is 60% of the Siberian tiger population in Country B. The population of Siberian tigers in Country C is 50% of that in Country A.

If the Siberian tiger population in Country C is 420, what is the Siberian tiger population in Country B?

A	B	C	D
1,400	1,200	1,000	1,600

Question 13

If transport emitted 6 million tons this year, and industrial emissions are the same as last year, what were the commercial emissions last year?

Carbon Emissions

| Last year | 15% | 10% | 20% | 25% | 30% |
| This year | 15% | 15% | 25% | 20% | 25% |

 Power Generation
Transport
Industrialisation
Commercial
Residential

A	B	C	D	E
11.5 million ton	10 million tons	3 million tons	12.5 million tons	8.5 million tons

Answer

Question 14

Points A and B are shown on the centimetre grid below (not to scale).

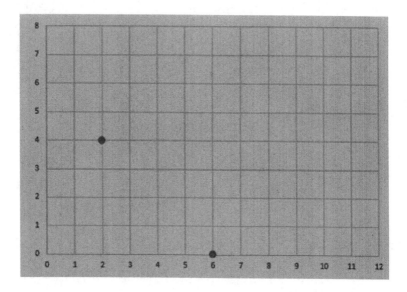

If you were to put another point at the co-ordinates (10, 4), what is the area of triangle made by each of the three points?

Answer

Question 15

Government spending on "Education services" and "Health services" was 56.3 billion pounds and 106.7 billion respectively for the year 2009-2010. In the same year, the Government spending on "Debt Interests" was

22.22% of the spending on "Education services", and the spending on "Education services", "Health services" and "Debt Interests" constituted 50% of the total spending by the Government.

What was the Government's approximate total spending for the year 2009-2010?

A	B	C	D
551 billion pounds	615 billion pounds	351 billion pounds	435 billion pounds

Answer

Question 16

The following graph shows the velocity of two cars at different times.

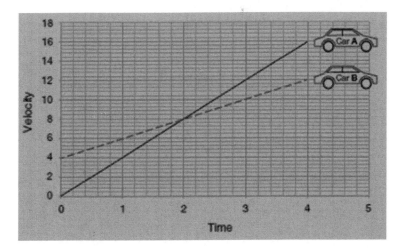

How much greater is the acceleration of Car A than the acceleration of Car B?

Acceleration (m/s2) = Change in velocity (m/s2) ÷ Change in time (s)

A	B	C	D
2 m/s2	4 m/s2	6 m/s2	8 m/s2

Answer

ANSWERS TO NUMERACY TEST

<u>Mental Arithmetic</u>

Q1. 0.25

Q2. 0.75

Q3. 20%

Q4. 8,550%

Q5. 20%

Q6. 40 miles

Q7. 168

Q8. 105

Q9. 24

Q10. 5/8

Q11. 348 pounds

Q12. 3 hours and 52 minutes

Interpreting and solving mathematics

Q1.

True

False

False

Q2.

False

False

True

Q3. 5.7

Q4. 64%

Q5. 64%

Q6. 28

Q7. 16%

Q8. 16.4

Q9. 594,000

Q10. 16,560,000

Q11. 44 hectares

Q12. 1,400

Q13. 12.5 million tons

Q14. 16cm squared

Q15. 351 billion pound

Q16. 2 m/s2

The Professional Skills Literacy Test

The QTS literacy test is a computer based assessment, which covers 4 different sections: spelling, punctuation, grammar and comprehension. You will take the spelling test first, before moving onto the other 3 sections. These sections can be completed in any order, however you cannot return back to the spelling section once it has been completed. The sections will be scored as follows:

- 10 marks for Spelling;

- 15 marks for Punctuation;

- 12 marks for Grammar;

- 12 marks for Comprehension.

While this can differ between years, it is estimated that you will need a minimum of 60% in order to pass this test. Now, let's look at the different sections of the test.

Spelling

During this exercise, you will be required to wear

headphones. There will be 10 sentences on the screen, with one word deleted from each sentence. You'll need to click on the deleted section to listen to the deleted word, before typing it into the space. You will be judged on the accuracy of your spelling.

Punctuation

This is an online test, although you won't be required to wear any headphones on this assessment. You will be given a passage or text with missing punctuation. You'll need to identify where to place a punctuation mark, where lower case letters should be turned to upper case and where a new paragraph should start. You won't be penalised for inserting correct punctuation where it is not necessary, but you won't be rewarded either.

Grammar

This is a multiple-choice assessment. You will be given a passage that is incomplete, with different bits of language missing. You will be required to make a grammatical decision about which piece of language (from the options given) should be inserted. You'll need to read the whole passage carefully, before making your choice.

Comprehension

This test requires you to read and analyse a passage, and then answer multiple choice questions. You will need to read the passage carefully, paying attention to the ideas expressed in the passage, the arguments and the tone of the speaker. You will need to make astute assumptions or judgements based on the content, and perform tasks such as:

- Identifying the meaning of words;

- Evaluating statements;

- Matching text with answer options;

- Identifying motivations.

PRACTICE TEST - LITERACY

SPELLING

*For the purpose of this assessment, please hand over this guide to somebody else. They will need to use **Appendix B** (*contained at the back of the book*).

They will need to read out each sentence, and you will need to write the correct spelling of the word that is missing in the sentence.*

SPELLING 1 The teacher knew what she was doing. She was a _____.

SPELLING 2 I had to _____ all kinds of problems.

SPELLING 3 He was a _____, old man.

SPELLING 4 I was _____ for my handwriting.

SPELLING 5 I tried to prevent any _____ from happening.

SPELLING 6 The young girl sounded

_____.

SPELLING 7 The child _____
all expectations.

SPELLING 8 It was a difficult _____
to make.

SPELLING 9 _____ was key.

SPELLING 10 Her work was _____.

PUNCTUATION

For the following 15 questions, rewrite the sentence, adding in the correct punctuation, capital letters and/or creating a new paragraph if required.

Question 1

the question is should we ban violent video games violent video games are often disputed in the media and the public regarding the impact they have on the younger generation

_____
_____
_____
_____
_____
_____
_____

Question 2

of all the ways to test immigrants looking to gain british citizenship, the life in the uk test might be the most absurd this is a test which relies on an extensive knowledge of the history of the united kingdom as someone who is not patriotic i find the idea of citizenship to be a fairly barren concept

_____
_____
_____
_____
_____
_____
_____

Question 3

as a regular zoo goer and enthusiast i have always been at odds with the idea of how would we like it if someone did this to us this is a very flawed concept but one that do gooders seem to have adopted as a mantra when it comes to animals

_____
_____
_____
_____
_____
_____
_____

Question 4

one of the most popular topics of debate is on whether the sale of cigarettes should be banned altogether these cancer causing sticks are one of the biggest points of contention for the global health services

_____

_____

_____

_____

_____

_____

_____

Question 5

for years rumours have persisted over the survival of one of the romanov children. disney even made a movie about it Anastasia in recent years however this has all been proven as a myth

_____

_____

_____

_____

_____

_____

_____

Question 6

wasps are undeniably aggressive and seek to monopolise territory and any food that is brought into their domain that being said however there are many misconceptions about the wasp

_____

_____

_____

_____

_____

_____

_____

Question 7

the long goodbye is regarded by some to be the finest of all chandlers works published in 1953 the book focuses on the character of philip marlowe and is the 6th book in the marlowe series.

_____

_____

_____

_____

_____

_____

_____

Question 8

are the human race really that aesthetically orientated i cannot pretend that ive never spent lots of money on something that looks nice before but a diamond is so small

_____

_____

_____

_____
_____
_____

GRAMMAR

For the following 8 questions, determine which sentence is grammatically correct. Please note, these questions are not an exact replica of the questions on your assessment, but they will test the same skills.

Question 1

A - They was going to be in big trouble.

B - They were going to be in big trouble.

C - They is going to be in big trouble.

D - Their going to be in big trouble.

Answer

[   ]

Question 2

A - I don't know were I am going.

B - I dont know where I am going.

C - I don't know where I am going.

D - I don't know wear I am going.

Answer

[   ]

Question 3

A - The sun raises early in the morning.

B - The sun rises early in the morning.

C - The sun roses early in the morning.

D - The sun rised early in the morning.

Answer

Question 4

A - You should lay down and go to sleep.

B - You should ly down and go to sleep.

C - You should lie down and go to sleep.

D - You should lye down and go to sleep.

Answer

Question 5

A - I were scared.

B - I was scared.

C - I is scared.

D - I wear scared.

Answer

```
┌─────────────────────────┐
│                         │
└─────────────────────────┘
```

Question 6

A - My coursework is better now than before.

B - My coursework was better now than before.

C - My coursework was better now then before.

D- My coursework is better now then before.

Answer

```
┌─────────────────────────┐
│                         │
└─────────────────────────┘
```

Question 7

A - Nobody I know have done a skydive.

B- No body I know have done a skydive.

C - No body I know has done a skydive.

D - Nobody I know has done a skydive.

Answer

```
┌─────────────────────────┐
│                         │
└─────────────────────────┘
```

Question 8

A - I really doesn't know how to do this.

B - I really don't know how to do this.

C - I really does know how to do this.

D - I really haven't know how to do this.

Answer

```
┌─────────────────────────────┐
│                             │
└─────────────────────────────┘
```

COMPREHENSION

Read the following passages and answer the questions that follow. Please note, these questions are not in the same style as your actual assessment, but will test the same skills required to pass this section of the Professional Skills Test.

Style is one of the deepest and most difficult subjects in writing. For some people, it takes years to develop this, and when they do, they must hone it to perfection. But what is style? And how do you know when you have found it?

My answer to all of these questions, is to encourage you to pick up your favourite book, and work out what it is about the writing that you like so much. Whether it's the sentence structure, the choice of words or the way the words make you feel – style is a deliberate, time-consuming but hugely worthwhile investment on the part of the writer. Unfortunately, this seems to be lost on many modern readers. With great style comes great literary integrity. Respect is invaluable – it's earned not by writing bad erotic fiction, but by honing your craft to the Nth degree. Make every word count. The uncomfortable truth is that most of us, indirectly at least, are guilty of homage or pastiche. Everything that could have been done has been done before, but as modern writers it is our job to better the past and create a new and exciting literary future. Remember, the author who looks at his book and says, 'nothing here can be improved' is out of aces. There is always something that can be bettered. To conclude, style represents a gargantuan, personal and in some ways selfish commitment, but it's one that any serious author needs to think about making. At the highest levels, literary respect can only be earned. If this is what you desire, then never forget that your craft is infinitely more valuable than your bank balance.

1. What is the overall argument that the speaker is trying to make?

A – Writers shouldn't care about making money.

B – Style is an essential quality for any serious writer.

C – Modern readers are shallow.

D – Writers should never be satisfied with their work.

Answer

```
┌─────────────────────────┐
│                         │
└─────────────────────────┘
```

2. What is the main reason that the author contrasts craft with bank balance?

A – She believes that craft and financial reward are mutually exclusive.

B – She believes that craft and financial reward can only be achieved via hard work.

C – She believes that writers should be more concerned with the quality of their work than how much money they are making from it.

D – She believes that writers who aren't concerned with how much money they are making are unrealistic.

Answer

```
┌─────────────────────────┐
│                         │
└─────────────────────────┘
```

3. In paragraph 3, what does the author mean by 'out of aces'?

A – Someone who is exceedingly arrogant.

B – Someone who is deluded about the quality of their own work.

C – Someone who is not very good at cards.

D – Someone who has run out of ideas on how to improve their work.

Answer

4. In the context of this passage, what is the meaning behind the phrase 'uncomfortable truth', as used in the third paragraph?

A – To show that all writers are guilty of homage in some way or other.

B – To show that all writers feel guilty about writing homage or pastiche.

C – To show that while all writers produce homage or pastiche, many of them are uncomfortable in the knowledge that they are doing so.

D – To show that most writers produce homage or pastiche, and therefore are not producing 'original ideas'.

Answer

The practice of illegally downloading music has been around for many years now, and shows little sign of slowing down. Despite increased attempts from record labels and artists alike to prevent people from listening without paying, the cancer continues to grow. By the late 2020s, it is estimated that overall artist profits will have declined by at least a third. This is having an inimical impact on the music industry. The problem with preventative strategies is that every time a new idea to stop the spread is introduced, new programmes rise up to defeat this. Technology and sharing software means that it's almost impossible to stop people from sharing their music with friends, and this inevitably leads to the same music then being shared online; at the artist's expense. While authorities have had substantial success in removing hard download links, i.e. people sharing music albums via RAR files or torrent links, it is extremely difficult to monitor the biggest medium of all – YouTube. Every day, thousands of songs are posted on YouTube. Downloaders have responded to this by creating programmes which allow you to download these songs from YouTube as an MP3 sound file. Even with the creation of ethical cheaper sharing programmes which generate a profit for the artist, hundreds of thousands of people continue to use illegal file download programmes every day. After all, why pay when you could get the files for free?

5. What is the meaning of the word 'inimical'?

A – Beneficial to a wide number of parties.

B – Beneficial to a singular party.

C – Harmful.

D – Apocalyptic.

Answer

[   ]

6. The author refers to illegal downloading as a cancer. What does he mean by this?

A – Illegal downloading is spreading like a harmful disease and is slowly killing the music industry.

B – Illegal downloading is comparable to mutated cells, spreading around the internet.

C – Illegal downloading is something that needs to be blasted with chemotherapy, before it's too late.

D – There is still no cure for illegal downloading.

Answer

[   ]

7. What does the author believe is the biggest problem for those trying to stop illegal downloads from happening?

A – YouTube.

B – New programmes are constantly being developed that make it easy to rip music from websites.

C – The creation of paid, ethical music sharing programmes.

D – The ability to download RAR files and torrents from the internet.

Answer

[   ]

8. The author finishes the paragraph by stating 'After all, why pay when you could get the files for free?' What is the name for this type of literary device?

A – Yes/No question.

B – Rhetorical question.

C – Onomatopoeia.

D – Irony.

Answer

[   ]

ANSWERS TO LITERACY TEST

Spelling

*Check **Appendix B** for correct spellings of the words.*

Punctuation

Q1. The question is: 'should we ban violent video games?' Video games are often disputed in the media, and by the public, regarding the impact they have on the younger generation.

Q2. Of all the ways to test immigrants looking to gain British Citizenship, the Life in the UK test might be the most absurd. This is a test which relies on an extensive knowledge of the history of the United Kingdom.

As someone who is not patriotic, I find the idea of citizenship to be a fairly barren concept.

Q3. As a regular zoo-goer and enthusiast, I have always been at odds with the idea of 'how would we like it if someone did this to us?' This is a very flawed concept, but one that do-gooders seem to have adopted as a mantra when it comes to animals.

Q4. One of the most popular topics of debate is on whether the sale of cigarettes should be banned altogether. These cancer-causing sticks are one of the biggest points of contention for the global health services.

Q5. For years, rumours have persisted over the survival of one of the Romanov children. Disney even made a movie about it, Anastasia. In recent years however, this has all been proven as a myth.

Q6. Wasps are undeniably aggressive and seek to monopolise territory and any food that is brought into their domain. That being said however, there are many misconceptions about the wasp.

Q7. The Long Goodbye is regarded by some to be the finest of all Chandler's works. Published in 1953, the book focuses on the character of Philip Marlowe and is the 6th book in the Marlowe series.

Q8. Are the human race really that aesthetically orientated? I cannot pretend that I've never spent lots of money on something that looks nice before, but a diamond is so small!

Grammar

Q1. B = They were going to be in big trouble

Q2. C = I don't know where I am going.

Q3. B = The sun rises early in the morning.

Q4. C = You should lie down and go to sleep.

Q5. B = I was scared.

Q6. A = My coursework is better now than before.

Q7. D = Nobody I know has done a skydive.

Q8. B = I really don't know how to do this.

Comprehension

Q1. B = Style is an essential quality for any serious writer.

The author's main argument is that style will hugely increase the quality of a writer's work. Therefore, it is inevitable that he believes style is an essential quality for any serious writer.

Q2. C = He believes that writers should be more concerned with the quality of their work than how much money they are making from it.

The writer states that 'your craft is infinitely more valuable than your bank balance'. This shows that he is someone who values the quality of work over how much money the work is making.

Q3. D = Someone who has run out of ideas on how to improve their work.

The term 'out of aces' in this context refers to someone who is out of ideas/improvements to make; aces being the highest ranked in a pack of cards.

Q4. D = To show that most writers produce homage or pastiche, and therefore are not producing 'original ideas'.

Answer option D is the only option that refers to 'most writers' rather than 'all writers'. Furthermore, Answer D is the only option which specifically refers to the problem with producing pastiche, making it an uncomfortable truth.

Q5. C = Harmful

The word inimical refers to something that is harmful, hostile or obstructing. The author believes that illegal downloading is harmful to the music industry.

Q6. A = Illegal downloading is spreading like a harmful disease and is slowly killing the music industry.

The speaker states that 'the cancer continues to grow'. This is reference to it spreading, and he follows this up by stating that the 'disease' is having a harmful impact upon the music industry.

Q7. B = New programmes are constantly being developed that make it easy to rip music from websites.

The author clearly states that 'the problem with preventative strategies is that every time a new idea to stop the spread is introduced, new programmes rise up to defeat this.'

Q8. B = Rhetorical question.

A rhetorical question is a question used to make a point rather than to elicit an answer. In this case, the author is trying to make the point that illegally downloading files is immoral, but at the same time is free and easy for everyone to do.

Chapter 9
Teacher Interview

Earlier in this guide, we told you about how our PGCE candidate (Mark) was taking 2 teacher interviews.
In this chapter, we are going to provide you with everything that you need to know in order to ACE your teacher interview, and secure your position in a school.

Interviews are always tricky, no matter what job you are applying for. This is especially the case for schools. Along with being asked interview questions, in many cases you will actually be asked to conduct/teach a practice lesson. Earlier in this guide, we provided you with a lesson planning kit. Use this in your interview preparation! Remember also that when you are being interviewed for a teaching position, you aren't just being interviewed for any job. Teachers aren't just teachers; they are carers and role models, and therefore it's essential that schools choose the right candidate for the job. Not only is it important that they select someone who can set an example to children, but they also need someone with the right personality. Teaching isn't easy. In fact, teaching is very hard indeed. The last thing that a school wants is to employ someone who will crumble under pressure when faced with a class full of students. With this in mind, they need to make sure that they have a personality that fits with the role. Throughout this chapter, we'll be showing you how to put this across in your answers.

In this chapter, we won't just cover interviewing for an actual teaching post. You might recall us mentioning that in order to gain a place on a teaching course, you'll often need to be interviewed by a senior member of staff. This chapter will cover this topic too, to ensure that you have all of your interview bases covered before you start applying for places.

<u>Let's start out with a reminder of the core competencies of teaching:</u>

Listening. Listening is absolutely essential for teachers. Part of the difficulty of teaching is that there are just so many different voices in the classroom. It's hard to know who to listen to and at what moments. Even one-to-ones can be challenging, because children in particular don't always make clear exactly what they are trying to say. This is why you need to be able to listen to what your pupils are saying. Remember that they will learn from your responses.

Relationship management. Next, we have relationship management. Teaching isn't just about adhering to curriculum material, it's about resolving conflict in the classroom and encouraging pupils to get along and grow as people. Particularly when you are teaching younger students, you are teaching them personal skills which will be essential later in life. If you've been to school, you'll probably be aware of the fact that conflict is inevitable in the classroom. Adolescents or teenagers are under huge amounts of pressure and this generates tension. Not everyone gets along. You must be able to prevent situations like this from getting out of hand, and act as a calm and unbiased support figure.

Instructing. Teachers teach! Instructing is what teaching is all about, so it goes without saying that this is a very important competency to have. You must be able to share your wisdom with pupils, in a clear and engaging manner. Your knowledge is a fantastic tool, but it's no good if you can't use it to full effect. Your ability to instruct will impact hugely upon the quality of your lessons, and can mean the difference between a perfect lesson and a class spiralling out of control. Teaching is a rollercoaster of emotions. Often, it can seem as if classes will ebb, flow and crumble regardless of how you behave or not; but this isn't the case. The truth is much more subtle than this, and it all comes down to how you, the teacher, conduct yourself.

Organisation. Organisation is arguably the most important competency for any teacher to have. The reality is that teaching is extremely stressful. If you don't keep on top of things then you will quickly become overwhelmed by the sheer volume of tasks on your plate. From lesson planning to marking, you will find yourself up against it timewise. This is why time management is an essential part of good organisation. Once you become a teacher, you'll realise why it was so frustrating when students talked or wasted time in your lessons. Every second is precious to teachers. Organisation will help you to save time, and get things done efficiently. This won't just be great for your students, but for your own peace of mind. It's important that you can minimise stress, so that you can get the best out of yourself.

Lesson Planning. Lesson planning is something that you will learn over the course of your training, and is an essential skill to have in your locker. There are two factors that decide how well a lesson is run – your planning and your leadership skills. If you haven't planned the lesson properly, then the quality of the class will suffer as a result. Students need organisation and discipline, not just to keep them in line, but to keep them occupied. Think about it. Would you come into a class and tell the students to just get on with whatever they want? No, you need a clear set of exercises and a structure to the lesson, which occupies their time and helps them to learn. No two days are the same as a teacher, you can't micromanage every single class to go in exactly the way that you want it to, but the more detailed your planning, the better.

Professionalism. Teachers are there to provide an example for their pupils, and therefore they must be able to look up to you. This means that your behaviour both inside and out of the classroom needs to be exemplary. You must be able to act with integrity, and show a good level of respect to everyone that you meet. As a teacher, an important part of your role is in practicing fairness and equality; and showing students the right way to behave.

Leadership. As the teacher, you are the leader of the class. You are someone whom students look up to, who they receive guidance from and will also act as an authority figure for the group. This means that you need to be able to live up to this role. If your students respect you, you'll have a far easier time teaching them. Leadership involves almost all of the competencies on this list, and is a fundamental quality for teachers to have!

What kind of questions will I be asked?

So, at this point you are probably wondering exactly what kind of questions you'll be asked in a teaching interview, and how these relate to the core competencies. The reality is that there is no set structure for a teaching interview. Unlike assessment-based interviews for services such as the Police; the nature of the questioning will largely depend upon a) the role that you are applying for, and b) the institution itself.

However, you can generally expect the structure of the interview questions to be in the following manner:

Part 1

Questions based around your interest in the role, what you know about the institution and your personality.

In this section of the interview, you'll be asked questions based around your research into the position, and your personality. It's common practice for most interviews, regardless of the position that you are applying for, to have a 'getting to know you' section. However, this section is even more important in the teacher interview.

This is because you will working with vulnerable people, of a young age. You'll need to pass a DBS check anyway in order to gain a position as a teacher, but the school still need to be certain of your personality. They don't just need to know that you are safe and trustworthy, but that you are reliable, hardworking, organised and able to cope under pressure.

Part 2

Questions based around your previous experience and subject knowledge.

In this section of the interview, you'll be asked questions based around your previous experience with schools or teaching, and your subject knowledge. By the latter, this doesn't mean they'll quiz you on specific topics, but they'll want to know the extent of your knowledge and whether there are any noticeable gaps. There is a good chance that before applying, you'll be given a copy of the curriculum to read through, so if you see anything that you are unfamiliar with or are noticeably weak in; this is the time to mention it.

Your previous experience is also extremely important. The interviewer will ask you questions based around the core competencies. For example, you might be asked to talk about a time when you have demonstrated a particular quality. When answering situational questions such as the above, we recommend using the STAR method:

<u>THE Star Method</u>

The **STAR** method works most effectively when preparing responses to situational type interview questions. It ensures that your responses to the interview questions follow a concise and logical sequence and also makes sure that you cover every possible area.

Situation – At the start of your esponse, you should explain what the situation was and who else was involved. This should be relatively comprehensive, so that the interview fully understands the scenario.

Task – Next explain what the task was. This will basically be an explanation of what had to be done and by whom.

Action – Then move on and explain what action you specifically took, and also what action other people took.

Result – Finally, explain what the result was following your actions. It is important to make sure that the result was positive as a direct result of your behaviour.

Using this method not only shows your thought process for each response, but it allows you to take the time and think carefully about each step in the process of your response.

Let's start off by looking at some typical 'personality-based' questions. These types of question can apply for both training course interviews, and for actual positions. You can be certain that training course providers will ask you plenty of questions based around your personality too, as they want to be sure that they are taking on the right type of person. You can expect this set of questions to involve questions surrounding your research into the role too.

On the next few pages, we've included a whole range of sample questions for you to practice with.

<u>Example Personality Questions</u>

Question 1.

Tell me a bit more about yourself.

This is the most common starting question. It's an opportunity for you to talk about your background, interest in the role and demonstrate your personality, all in one go. Your answer to this question shouldn't be too long, but at the same time you still need to give the interviewers an encouraging insight into who you are as a person and why you are suitable for the position.

Remember that teachers need to be liberal and stable. The school must be able to trust you with their students. This means that you should keep things on topic, and don't tell them about anything inappropriate. For example, it would be a good idea to tell the interviewers about how you like to help out at your local golf club on Sundays, but not to tell them about how you go out every night and spend your wages in the casino. This will show them that you are irresponsible. If you can't look after your own affairs in a sensible manner, then why should they give you responsibility for their pupils?

On the next page, we've left a space for you to write out your own answer to this question. Have a go at this, and then compare it to the sample answer below the box.

You'll notice that throughout all of our example responses, we've tried to mix things up. This means that in some responses, we'll be responding as if we were applying for a training course, and in some responses we'll be responding as if we were applying for a real teaching position.

Q1. Tell me a bit more about yourself.

<u>Sample Response</u>

'I'm a confident, enthusiastic and responsible person, with a passion for improving the lives of others. I recently completed my degree in English and American Literature, and now I would love the opportunity to put my knowledge into further practice.

In the past month, I have spent an extensive period volunteering and observing in a local secondary school. My duties included assisting students with the English learning material, helping various teachers to deliver presentations and I even had a couple of one-to-one sessions with experienced professionals in the department, so that I could gain an insight into what it takes to become a successful English teacher. I have previously worked in a library, helping younger children to select their first books. I feel that this gave me crucial experience with the bracket of people I would be working with whilst training to become a teacher. Furthermore, I am excited to be able to work with like-minded colleagues and professionals on your course, who share my passion for helping others and educating.

I believe that my personality and experience make me a tremendous fit for your course, and that I will one day become an excellent teacher.'

Question 2.

What is it that has attracted you to this school/course specifically?

This is another common question, and one that requires you to have researched the school or course before applying. Just as any employer would be, schools are wary of candidates who are just applying to each and any organisation hoping to gain a job. They want someone who truly cares about their cause. Showing that you have researched the position and the school, and have found aspects that you value, will go a long way to demonstrating that you are interested and enthusiastic about applying. This doesn't mean that you need to go overboard. You just need to find certain qualities or values about the organisation or course, and then match them with your own.

When you are researching schools or courses, make sure you have a clear idea of their learning ethos. Write this down (in simple terms), before making a list of your own qualities. Now, work out how your qualities match up to the learning ethos of the school. For example, if the school is particularly passionate about improving the ICT skills of its students, make sure you highlight your own expertise in ICT and what you could bring/add to this.

This isn't just a question about the school either. By default, the interviewer is also asking about the position you are applying for. Make sure you list something specific or appealing about the responsibilities and job description, which makes it worthwhile for you.

On the next page, we've left a space for you to write out your own answer to this question. Have a go at this, and then compare it to the sample answer below the box.

Q2. What is it that has attracted you to this school/ course specifically?

Sample Response

'Before applying for this position, I conducted extensive research into your school. I was absolutely delighted with what I found. I believe that the learning ethos of your organisation closely matches my own. In particular, I was impressed with this school's attitude towards extra-curricular learning. I can see that you take a real initiative towards getting your pupils engaged in learning outside of school hours, and I think this is really commendable. Although I greatly enjoyed my time working in other schools, I have always felt like this was something lacking, and the same could be said about my own schooling years. If I was employed in this position, this is something I'd really like to get involved in. I don't just want to teach, but I want to help pupils enjoy learning. Learning shouldn't be a chore, it should be something that children want to do.

In regards to the role itself, I believe this would present me with a number of exciting opportunities. I've looked at the English curriculum via your school website and the material on the list is absolutely perfect for me. I've covered every single one of the topics either during my degree or at A-Level and GCSE. With a quick refresh, I'd be ready to teach these subjects to anyone, at any time! Having spoken to one of the teachers in your department, to discuss the responsibilities that your staff members hold, I can safely say that I am more than up for the challenge.'

> **Question 3**.
>
> Why do you think that you would be a good fit for this position/course?

This is your chance to tell the employers why they should hire you! It might seem like a scary topic, but it's actually a really good question for you. You know your own strengths better than anyone, so show them to the interviewer! As we said in the last question, match up your own abilities with the position that you are applying for. Why is this a good position for you, and why are you a good fit for their school or course in general?

When you are answering this question, make sure you use plenty of positive terminology. Words such as enthusiastic, dedicated, committed, caring and responsible will go a long way to showing the interviewer why they should choose you. You can also (albeit briefly) use your own experience in this question. For example, mentioning the fact that you have worked in a school or college before, to demonstrate that you already have knowledge and experience.

One big mistake that many people make when answering this question is that they go overboard, trying to convince the interviewer of how strong a candidate they are. They don't keep their qualities specific to the role, or even focus too hard on how they would be a good fit for the wider organisation. Remember that listening is one of the core competencies of teaching. This question is asking you about the position you are applying for, not the school in general. Keep references to the latter to a minimum.

On the next page, we've left a space for you to write out your own answer to this question. Have a go at this, and then compare it to the sample answer below the box.

Q3. Why do you think that you would be a good fit for this position/course?

<u>Sample Response</u>

'I believe that I would be an excellent fit for this course. There are several reasons for this.

Primary amongst these reasons, is my skillset. Having taken English for my degree, I can safely say that I meet the required educational qualities in abundance. I have a deep understanding of English Literature, having also obtained strong grades in GCSE and A-Level, and I believe that teaching the subject would be a natural culmination of these studies. The consistently strong marks that I obtained throughout my education are proof of this.

I also have fantastic leadership qualities. Time and time again throughout my degree, I have demonstrated this. I have taken leadership of many group projects, playing a leading role in each group, achieving great marks. I take responsibility for the actions of others, and am never content to rest on my laurels and let other members of my team fail. I strongly believe in the value of helping others to succeed too, and learning in the process.

Finally, I already have experience of working in a school. I've gone out of my way to obtain and make the most of this experience, and this gives me a crucial advantage going into the course. I already have a great idea of what to expect and this means that nerves won't play a part when it comes to placement. I'm ready for the challenges ahead.'

Question 4.

What are your biggest weaknesses?

If you've interviewed for a job before, you'll probably be familiar with this (dreaded) question. The reality is that this question isn't as hard as it sounds, and you shouldn't be scared to give an honest answer, as long as this isn't an answer that will strongly interfere with your ability to do the job.

The trick is to make your weaknesses sound positive. The majority of people will tell you that the best answer to this question is, 'I'm a perfectionist' but these days, the interviewers will almost expect you to answer like this. A good answer to this question will tell the truth, but still make it clear that you are willing to learn and improve.

Remember that in order to become a teacher, you'll need to be constantly reflecting on your own practice and how you can improve. This means that you'll need a strong level of personal awareness. Don't tell the interviewer that you have no weaknesses, because this simply isn't true, and they won't believe you. There is always something that you can improve on, and it's your responsibility to do this, for your pupils and for the school.

On the next page, we've left a space for you to write out your own answer to this question. Have a go at this, and then compare it to the sample answer below the box.

Q4. What are your biggest weaknesses?

<u>Sample Response</u>

'Great question! I would say that my biggest weakness is that I still get quite nervous speaking in front of large numbers of people. Although I have had a lot of practice with this since university, and job placements, I feel as though this is an area I can really work and improve on. Obviously, I understand how important it is to communicate effectively to a class full of students, and therefore I am continuously working on speaking in front of lots of people. A good example of this is recently, where I spoke in front of a crowd at my local golf club. I took part in an awards evening, and gave a speech to a room full of people. This was fairly terrifying, but I was congratulated at the end of the speech by various people in the room and received a round of applause. From this, I realised that despite my nerves, I am actually quite good at public speaking, and with a bit more confidence and practice, I think I will, in time, become an effective public speaker.'

Question 5.

How would you define 'success'?

This is an interesting question, and the answer will tell the school a great deal about your personality. It will show them how ambitious you are, your plans for the future and how dedicated/committed you are to the cause. Of course, every answer will be subjective to the person answering, and there is no real right or wrong answer to this.

You should avoid going overboard, for example telling them that for you, success would mean being the principal of the school. Similarly, however, the school want to know that you won't be satisfied with minor success. Don't tell them that for you, success means having a quiet and well performing class. This will indicate that you are happy with a job half done. You can also show that you understand success for teachers is only ever short term, as there are always challenges to be met and new obstacles around the corner. The beauty of teaching is that for all of the challenges, there will be uplifting success stories, and you can use these challenges and successes to keep you motivated.

On the next page, we've left a space for you to write out your own answer to this question. Have a go at this, and then compare it to the sample answer below the box.

Q5. How would you define 'success'?

<u>Sample Response</u>

'For me, success is really difficult to define. As a teacher, I would like to think that success means having all of your students achieve top marks in their exams, and being completely happy while doing so. However, I know that it's never that simple.

Long term success can be achieved but it's subjective to every single student. You might succeed with one student but have another who struggles, or fails to grasp the message. As a teacher you are naturally faced with a huge number of students and consequently many different problems to deal with. Given that teachers take on new classes every year, it's impossible to say you've achieved long term success on a collective basis, because there are always new challenges and students that come up.

With this in mind, I believe that success means knowing that I have done my utmost to improve the learning and personal potential of all my students. I am someone who always gives 150% to every single task and I will carry this into teaching. I'm extremely dedicated and will do my utmost to change my classes for the better. I want to make a difference in their lives.'

Question 6.

How are your time management skills?

As we've mentioned, time management is an essential skill for any teacher to have. Therefore, it's inevitable that you'll be questioned on this during the interview.

In this example, the questioners aren't asking you to give a specific example, however you will obviously need to elaborate further; and it would be helpful for you to a) acknowledge that you have great time management skills, b) show that you know why these are important for teachers, and c) demonstrate briefly when you have used them.

Don't just show the interviewers that you have time management skills, but why they are important. Teaching is about going above and beyond what is generally expected, and you should take the same attitude to your interview answers.

On the next page, we've left a space for you to write out your own answer to this question. Have a go at this, and then compare it to the sample answer below the box.

Q6. How are your time management skills?

Sample Response

'I am happy to say that my time management skills are exceptional. Throughout my degree, I have had to use these skills to good effect on a number of occasions, particularly where deadlines are concerned.

I understand that time management is one of the most important qualities that any teacher can have. Teachers have a hectic and stressful working life, and time management is something that can really help with this. It is our responsibility as teachers to manage our time effectively, as this will have short and long term benefits for our students. The better organised the teacher, the better they will be able to deliver their lessons to students in an efficient, calm and clear manner.

I have not only used time management skills at university, but in my other areas of work, too. Particularly during my work experience at local schools, I made a point of being extremely organised, and picked up some top organisational tips from the professionals around me. I believe that I would have no issues with this if I was to be offered a place on your course.'

Example Competency Based Questions

Question 7.

Can you tell me about a time when you have personally helped to deal with a particularly difficult student?

Obviously, if you are an NQT, then the interviewers won't expect you to have dealt with something like this yourself (although if you have then by all means use this in your response!) However, they will have expected you to have experience in the classroom and school environment before. By default, this usually means that you'll have dealt with at least one problematic or badly behaved student in the past.

In your response, you should show the interviewers the actions that YOU personally took in order to resolve and deal with the situation. Even if you simply assisted the lead teacher in dealing with this, make sure you draw attention to your role and how you were imperative to mending the situation.

As you go through your response, make sure you use the STAR method. Start off with the situation/problem and then work your way through in a structured manner. Not only will this make it easier for you to narrate your answer, but it will help the interviewers to understand exactly what took place and what you did to help resolve it.

On the next page, we've left a space for you to write out your own answer to this question. Have a go at this, and then compare it to the sample answer below the box.

Q7. Can you tell me about a time when you have personally helped to deal with a particularly difficult student?

Sample Response

'When I was taking work experience at my previous school, I was assigned to observe and help with a Year 9 English class. The teacher in charge was a highly experienced professional, who had been teaching at the school for over 20 years. Unfortunately, in this class, there was one boy who simply refused to behave.

Halfway through the lesson, the class were assigned to do group work. The individual in question was placed in a group with 2 of his friends, and quickly started messing around. He was refusing to participate in the subject matter – Shakespeare. The teacher in question had been dealing with this kind of behaviour all year, and it seemed that she had simply had enough of it. She didn't want to deal with the student anymore and seemed to be ignoring him and his group, in favour of more well behaved students. I decided to sit down and try and get the boy and his friends to cooperate. They simply laughed at me. One of them pinged my cheek with a ruler. Frustrated, I took the teacher to one side and questioned her over why she was ignoring their bad behaviour. She informed me that she was not prepared to help students who simply didn't want to learn. After the class, I informed her that I felt this was unprofessional and that she should be reaching out to all students, regardless of their behaviour. She agreed with me and together we set out a plan to help the misbehaving students in the next lesson.

During the next lesson, I was given the role of personally helping the individual who was misbehaving. When it came to group work, he simply worked with me instead of with his friends. After encouraging him to try with the subject material, the boy confessed to me that he didn't understand the material and that is why he was misbehaving. In conjunction with his teacher, I arranged for him to take after school lessons with both me and a senior member of staff; to give him extra assistance. This worked extremely well and his bad behaviour quickly stopped.

I feel that my taking initiative and professional attitude really helped to resolve this situation and lead to a student who was better off.'

Question 8.

Teaching requires someone who is extremely flexible. Can you give me an example of a time when you have demonstrated your flexibility?

As a teacher, you need to be prepared for surprises, because you are going to get an awful lot of them. There will be times when you come into work and have planned out your entire day, before one incident throws a spanner in the works. School is a chaotic and often mad environment. You need to be able to adapt to a multitude of different situations, and keep a calm head under pressure. Not only this, but you need to be able to adjust your priorities according to what is happening around you. You might think that one student is your priority, but then another comes in with another issue that needs resolving. Likewise, in lessons you might find that the original plan you had for the class goes out of the window, because you made a mistake in the plan or overestimated the knowledge of the group. Incidents like this are extremely commonplace for teachers, and therefore you must be flexible enough to deal with them.

Interviewers need to be sure that you are someone who can cope with the demands of the job. Being flexible is a sign that you won't collapse under the pressure of teaching, and that you understand the need for adaptability in the chaotic classroom environment.

On the next page, we've left a space for you to write out your own answer to this question. Have a go at this, and then compare it to the sample answer below the box.

Q8. Teaching requires someone who is extremely flexible. Can you give me an example of a time when you have demonstrated your flexibility?

<u>Sample Response</u>

'I am a highly flexible person, who can adapt to any situation with ease. This was best demonstrated by my work experience in a local school. At the end of my work experience, I was invited by the teacher to actually lead the class for one of the group activities. I had planned the activity the night before, and was really excited to get things going.

Unfortunately, the activity did not go quite as I had planned it. While my instructions were clear, and organising the task went exactly to plan, it seemed that I had really overestimated the knowledge base of the class. The subject matter (despite being what we had learned) was pitched far too high and it quickly became apparent that the class simply hadn't understood what I was asking them to do. The result was confusion and in some cases, misbehaviour. I quickly realised the error of my ways, scrapped the task immediately and engaged the group in a subject-based discussion.

To my relief, this had an immediate positive impact. The class revelled in the opportunity to make their voices on the subject heard, and the result was a fun and engaging discussion which really brought out the enthusiasm of the group. At the end of the discussion, I asked individual members of the class to give me an account of things they had learned, which I then wrote down on the board. I managed to fill an entire side, before the teacher took over and continued on with the next exercise.

Overall, I was really pleased with the way that I managed

to think on my feet and demonstrate flexibility, as well as an ability to deviate constructively from my original plan.'

Question 9.

One of your English students has failed on his crucial end of year examination. With whom does the blame lie?

This is a slightly left field question, but the answer is very simple. It's your fault! As the teacher, it is your job to take responsibility for the student and his grades. If he has failed to achieve a good grade, then it's because you have failed to teach him properly. This might seem really unfair, and obviously it's never this black and white, but for the context of your answer you should assume responsibility. Don't blame it on the student, as this will come across badly to the interviewer.

Whilst taking responsibility, you should also go into detail about how you would rectify the situation. Given that there isn't too much information here, use your imagination! Explain why it's your fault as the teacher and not the fault of the student, the reasons that you have taken this stance and solutions to the problem. This will show that you aren't just someone who takes responsibility for problems, but someone who can work constructively and produce quick solutions. If you have actually had experience of this before then even better, you can tell the interviewers what happened and what you did/changed as a result of this.

On the next page, we've left a space for you to write out your own answer to this question. Have a go at this, and then compare it to the sample answer below the box.

Q9. One of your English students has failed on his crucial end of year examination. With whom does the blame lie?

Sample Response

'When a student fails to achieve an acceptable grade, the blame lies with the teacher. In this case, me. As teachers, it is our job to ensure that students are at a level where they feel both confident and knowledgeable enough to pass their exams. If this has happened, or they aren't in the right frame of mind to do so, then we have failed. While I appreciate that the actual taking of the exam is not under our control, this does not absolve us from responsibility when something like this happens.

If a student has failed to achieve an acceptable grade in their exam, I would do my utmost to ensure that this was fixed. Not only would I ask the student to attend afterschool and/or lunchtime based learning sessions with myself, but I would liase with support staff in the school; such as the student's form tutor. If I felt necessary, I would also contact their parents to discuss the possibility of tutoring.

I would be more than happy to give up my own free time, in order to ensure that the student got up to speed and could achieve a much higher grade in their next examination.'

Question 10.

Give me an example of a time when you have had to take criticism from a senior member of staff. How did you deal with this?

Teaching is about growing and developing yourself as a person, as well as an educator. As a trainee or NQT, it's important that you are someone who is able to take feedback constructively, and apply this to your own practice. When you start working in a school, you'll be surrounded by members of staff who have spent far more time teaching than you have. They'll have experience and knowhow in abundance, and you should take full advantage of this. When a senior member of staff criticises or provides you with feedback, listen to them. Take it on board, because you'll be grateful to have received their wisdom when things get tough.

As you might have guessed, a good answer to this question will tell the interviewer about a time when you have taken criticism constructively, and used this to improve your own practice.

On the next page, we've left a space for you to write out your own answer to this question. Have a go at this, and then compare it to the sample answer below the box.

Q10. Give me an example of a time when you have had to take criticism from a senior member of staff. How did you deal with this?

Sample Response

'When I was working as a trainee at my previous work experience placement, I was invited to lead a class in a group exercise. I spent the whole night preparing for the exercise, excited to have my chance to shine.

Unfortunately, the exercise did not go quite as I had planned it to. My instructions were very clear, but the class sensed weakness and started to misbehave. I could not get them under control and they refused to listen to me. Several members of the group started throwing things across the room. The exercise was a disaster and the students failed to learn anything. I was extremely disappointed with this.

During our debrief after the lesson, the teacher that I was working with explained to me that my mistake had been not laying down ground rules before the exercise started. That is to say, I should have told the class that I expect them to behave in a particular manner and that there would be consequences if not. Because I failed to do this, the class assumed that they could get away with bad behaviour, and the exercise failed as a result.

Two days later, I was asked to take another group exercise with the same class. I took on board the teacher's feedback and laid out the ground rules before the exercise started. The class behaved much better this time and the exercise was a fun and educational success. I was extremely pleased with this, and felt I had learned an important lesson about discipline.'

Conclusion

You have now reached the end of your *How To Become A Teacher* guide, and no doubt will feel more prepared to tackle the application process. We hope you have found this guide an invaluable insight into the process, and understand what will be required of you.

For any type of selection process, we believe there are a few things to remember in order to better your chances and increase your overall performance.

REMEMBER – THE THREE Ps!

Preparation. This may seem relatively obvious, but you will be surprised by how many people fail because they lacked preparation and knowledge. You want to do your utmost to guarantee the best possible chance of succeeding. Be sure to conduct as much preparation as possible prior to your assessment tests and interview, to ensure that you are 100% prepared.

Perseverance. You are far more likely to succeed at something if you continuously set out to achieve it. Everybody comes across setbacks or obstacles in their life. The important thing to remember when this happens, is to use those setbacks and obstacles as a way of progressing. It is what you do with your past experiences that helps to determine your success in the future. If you fail at something, consider 'why' you have failed. This will allow you to improve and enhance your performance for next time.

Performance. Your performance will determine whether or not you are likely to succeed. Attributes that are often associated with performance are *self-belief, motivation* and *commitment.* Self-belief is important for anything you do in life. It allows you to recognise your own abilities and skills and believe that you can do well. Believing that you can do well is half the battle! Being fully motivated and committed is often difficult for some people, but we can assure you that nothing is gained without hard work and determination. If you want to succeed, you will need to put in that extra time and hard work!

Work hard, stay focused, and you can achieve whatever you set your mind to!

Good luck with your teaching application, and with all your future endeavours.

The How2become team

APPENDIX

APPENDIX A

List of accredited providers for the Assessment Only route.

*Please note this is not a complete list of providers, and only includes providers with a listed contact number.

East of England

Billericay Educational Consortium - 01245 683619

Chiltern Training Group SCITT - 01582 599921

Norfolk Teacher Training Centre - 01603 773708

Pilgrim Partnership - 01234 408590

Suffolk and Norfolk ITT - 01603 307703

Tendring Hundred Primary SCITT - 01255 509646

The Bedfordshire Schools Training Partnership - 01462 817445

The Shire Foundation - 01582 522121

University of Bedfordshire - 01234 793047

University of Hertfordshire - 01707 285708

East Midlands

Bishop Grosseteste University - 01522 583729

CfBT Education Trust SCITT - 07919 568841

Educate Teacher Training - 01476 512797

Nottingham Trent University - 0115 848 4200

The Beauchamp ITT Partnership - 0116 272 9113

Greater London

Bromley Schools' Collegiate - 020 8300 6566

Goldsmiths, University of London - 020 7717 2245

Jewish Teacher Training Partnership - 020 8203 6427

Kingston University - 020 8417 5075

London Diocesan Board for Schools (LDBS) SCITT - 0207 932 1126

London Metropolitan University - 0207 133 2983

Middlesex University - 020 8411 5555

The Havering Teacher Training Partnership - 01708 255006

The Pimlico-London SCITT - 0207 802 3455

University of East London - 020 8223 2319

University of Greenwich - 020 8331 9000

Wandsworth Primary Schools' Consortium - 020 8772 9528

North East England

Carmel Teacher Training Partnership (CTTP) - 01325 254525

Northumbria University - 0191 215 6467

Southfields Academy teaching school SCITT - 020 8870 1797

University of Sunderland - 0191 515 2399

North West England

Edge Hill University - 01695 650832

Kingsbridge EIP SCITT - 01942 510712

Mersey Boroughs ITT Partnership - 0151 426 6869

North Manchester ITT Partnership - 0161 202 0161

University of Manchester - 0161 275 3461

South East England

Bourton Meadow Initial Teacher Training Centre - 01280 823374

Canterbury Christ Church University - 01227 782298

George Abbot SCITT - 01483 888070

Surrey South Farnham SCITT - 0800 073 4444

Thames Primary Consortium - 01268 570215

The Buckingham Partnership - 01280 827 316

The University of Buckingham - 01280 820219

University of Reading - 0118 378 2691

University of Southampton - 023 8059 4669

University of Sussex - 01273 877050

West Berkshire Training Partnership - 01635 42155

South West

Bath Spa University - 01225 875650

Cornwall School Centred Initial Teacher Training (Cornwall SCITT) - 01872 267092

Mid Somerset Consortium for Teacher Training - 01458 449418

The Learning Institute South West SCITT - 01726 891 745

University of Gloucestershire - 01242 714852

Wessex Schools Training Partnership - 01202 662044

West Midlands

Birmingham City University - 0121 331 4627

The Keele and North Staffordshire Primary SCITT -

01782 297360

The OAKS (Ormiston and Keele SCITT) - 01782 734332

Yorkshire and Humber

Bradford College - 01274 431680

Leeds City Teaching School Alliance - 01133 075432

Leeds Trinity University - 0113 283 7268

North Lincolnshire SCITT Partnership - 01724 297950

University of Hull - 01723 357240

APPENDIX B

Appendix B needs to be used in conjunction with the Professional Skills Chapter (Literacy – Spelling section).

For this paper, you will require the assistance of someone else. If you haven't passed the book over to someone else, please do so now!

<u>How to work through the paper:</u>

You will have to complete sentences and fill in the correct spelling of the word that is read out to you.

SPELLING 1

The word is **professional**.

*The teacher knew what she was doing. She was a **professional**.*

The word is **professional**.

SPELLING 2

The word is **encounter**.

*I had to **encounter** all kinds of problems.*

The word is **encounter**.

SPELLING 3

The word is **pretentious**.

*He was a **pretentious**, old man.*

The word is **pretentious**.

SPELLING 4

The word is **criticised**.

*I was **criticised** for my handwriting.*

The word is **criticised**.

SPELLING 5

The word is **arguments**.

*I tried to prevent any **arguments** from happening.*

The word is **arguments**.

SPELLING 6

The word is **sincere**.

*The young girl sounded **sincere**.*

The word is **sincere**.

SPELLING 7

The word is **exceeded**.

*The child **exceeded** all expectations.*

The word is **exceeded**.

SPELLING 8

The word is **decision**.

*It was a difficult **decision** to make.*

The word is **decision**.

SPELLING 9

The word is **perseverance**.

***Perseverance** is key.*

The word is **perseverance**.

SPELLING 10

The word is **abysmal**.

*Her work was **abysmal**.*

The word is **abysmal**.

PRACTICE TEACHER INTERVIEW QUESTIONS AND ANSWERS

How2Become have created this FANTASTIC teacher interview questions and answers guide to help you prepare for ANY interview during your teaching career.

Packed full of interview questions and sample responses, this guide is guaranteed to aid you during your preparation stages when applying to become a teacher.

Not only does this guide contain lots of sample interview questions, but we also demonstrate the core competencies that you need to be focusing on in order to score top marks in your teacher interview!

FOR MORE INFORMATION ON OUR CAREER GUIDES, PLEASE CHECK OUT THE FOLLOWING:

WWW.HOW2BECOME.COM

WHY NOT PRACTICE FOR YOUR QTS!

FOR MORE INFORMATION ON OUR CAREER AND EDUCATIONAL RESOURCES, PLEASE CHECK OUT THE FOLLOWING:

WWW.HOW2BECOME.COM

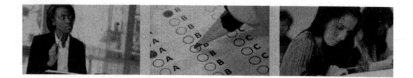

Get Access To
FREE
Psychometric
Tests

www.PsychometricTestsOnline.co.uk

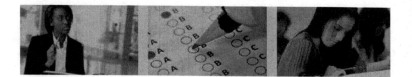